THE LAST I
EDI

Ninety years of cinema entertainment
in Scotland's capital city

By Brendon Thomas

MOORFOOT PUBLISHING
EDINBURGH   1984

© E.M. Thomas, 1984

ISBN 0 906606 09 8

Thomas, Brendon
  The last picture shows — Edinburgh.
  1. Moving-picture theaters — Scotland — Edinburgh
  (Lothian) — History. 2. Edinburgh (Lothian) — Theaters —
  History.
  791.43'09413'4   PN1993.5.G7

The publisher acknowledges subsidy from
  the Scottish Arts Council towards
  publication of this volume.

Published by:
  Moorfoot Publishing,
  PO Box 506,
  SW Postal District,
  Edinburgh 10.

Printed by:
  Kelso Graphics,
  The Knowes,
  Kelso.

CONTENTS

Operetta House (Demolition)

INTRODUCTION

BEFORE 1918 : TENTS AND POTTED PALMS

An old man's memory provides us with the only record of the first moving pictures in the Edinburgh area. These were shown in a booth in the Iona Street fairground, Leith, in 1893, and the story came to light in the reminiscences of Willie Salvona, a member of the town's fairground-owning family.

In 1963 Mr. Salvona told George Baird, Edinburgh's first cinema historian, that he recalled a Mr. Swallow renting a booth at the fairground and showing a film of a train at a level-crossing. It is not possible to say with certainty what kind of picture apparatus produced Swallow's show — if indeed it consisted of moving pictures at all. Twenty years earlier Edward Muybridge had invented his Zoopraxiscope, designed to show a horse in motion by flashing a series of still pictures, each slightly different from the one before, past the viewer's eyes. There were many improvements in the infant motion picture science in the twenty years after 1873, notably the production of celluloid film by Eastman and Blagny. However, the likelihood is that astonished Leithers were shown a pirated version of Edison's Kinetoscope.

The Kinetoscope was basically a peepshow affair, with the eye looking towards the source of light positioned behind the film. The light source was often insufficiently bright for adequate viewing and the frames flickered by at a rate of forty-six per second, causing considerable eyestrain. The first certain time and place of the Kinetoscope's use in Edinburgh was at H.E. Moss's Christmas Carnival in the Waverley Market in December 1894, later shown in a permanent hall for the first time in the city at Moss's Empire Palace Theatre in Nicolson Street on April 14th 1896. *The Scotsman's* reviewer pronounced it a flop : the pictures were too blurred, the movement too slow (the result of film frames flashing past at twice the speed of modern cine film) and "of too funereal a character" for showing a shoeblack, a cockfight, or a dance, all of them subjects of the minute-long films. On that occasion the new film entertainment shared the playbill with Professor Duncan's collie dogs performing a sketch about a fire-brigade rescue.

The Kinetoscope was being exhibited throughout Britain in competition with another film device, one destined to replace it completely — the Cinematograph. Invented by the Lumière brothers, who worked in their father's photographic factory in Lyons, the Cinematograph reached Paris in 1895, London on February 20th 1896 and Edinburgh (from Glasgow) on June 1st 1896. The projectionist for the entire tour was M. Trewey, formerly an elocutionist. *The Scotsman* pronounced the evening a success — "the light was perfect". In the Cinematograph the modern principle of cinema was established, a bright light being shone through the moving film, projecting it on to a separate screen. Flicker decreased with the reduction in the number of frames passing through the projector per second, about fifteen to eighteen being the usual number. The first film subjects had been chosen for their qualities of movement, providing images an audience could readily recognise — like workers leaving the Lumière factory or the arrival of a train at a station. Edinburgh probably saw some of the original Lumière programme and how these films were received can be guessed from the reactions of the citizens of Huddersfield and Blackburn when shown the same entertainment marvel. The patrons allegedly ducked in their seats when a gardener was sprayed with a water hose and some made for the exits when a train appeared to enter the auditorium!

While still being regarded as nothing more than a scientific toy, progress in motion picture development was rapid and on December 20th 1897 a three-dimensional show was unveiled at the Queen's Hall in Edinburgh's Queen Street (now the BBC studios). This was the Analyticon which consisted of two projectors superimposing pictures on a ten-foot screen, viewed with the use of an individual "analyst", a device like opera glasses. That evening the audience saw 3-D animals at the zoo and church interiors. Within two years a colour Analyticon was showing in the same hall a film of London by night. The promoter, T.J. West, also showed more conventional films, of the army, navy, and travel.

However the main growth area for film shows at the beginning of the century was the fairground. Many cinema-owning families started this way; for example, the Greens of Glasgow and Leith's Salvona family. In 1899 a tent in Jane Street, Leith, was called Falconer's Picture House, and may have been fairly typical of the state of the developing industry. Films, still only a minute or so in length, were often made by the showman himself. Filmed records of local events, sometimes shown on the same day, were always great favourites, as were those featuring newsworthy events — Gladstone's funeral, the Corbett-Fitzsimmons fight, a fraudulent mock-up of the Boer War. From France came films with more sophisticated, fictional, often sexual subjects, and Meliès, a former director of the Houdini Theatre in Paris, began to develop the situation film.

The mushrooming cinema industry was already finding good films difficult to come by, and French films in particular carried a hint of danger — to the exhibitor wary of offending public taste and falling foul of the authorities. For example in 1900

Georges Meliès produced *Les Nouvelles Luttes Extravagantes* in which two male wrestlers changed sex. The chaplain to the Showmen's Guild, who regarded himself as censor to the early cinema industry, later told the National Council of Public Morals in 1917:

"I remember the awful days of the uncensored funny pictures that came from France. Anyone connected (with the industry) must feel that the improvement has been so great and so continuous that there is no serious cause for any censure or serious alarm at the present state of affairs."

A couple of years into the new century, three entertainment names well-known in Edinburgh were touring the country with films in their repertoires. They were T.J. West with his Modern Marvel Company (often seen at the Queen's Hall), Ralph Pringle of the North American Animated Picture Company (later to settle in Grove Street and Elm Row) and Charles W. Poole with his Myriorama. Green, later based in Glasgow, was also nomadic, owning £8,000-worth of touring equipment including a steam organ. But the Cinematograph Act of 1909 effectively took the film show out of the fairground and into the cinema once and for all.

The Cinematograph Act was passed none too soon. Already, flat hall floors, cricked necks, fleas, and the headaches caused by projection flicker, made cinema a poor man's entertainment. Even worse, a booth could not offer reasonable resistance to fire, and a conflagration was always a possibility in the presence of highly flammable nitrate film combined with strong lighting. Public enthusiasm had waned for a while, entertainment investors following public taste into roller skating, which had last been a craze in the 1880s. Film booths closed while skating rinks opened, one example being the Olympia, Annandale Street, owned by F.A. Lumley and J. Maguire, future Edinburgh cinema owners. Pringle's, Elm Row, was both a roller-skating rink and a cinema. However the skating craze did not last long and rinks often then became cinemas, as in the case of the Olympia.

The Act required the projection booth to be separate from the auditorium and laid down minimum fire precautions which local by-laws made even tighter. As a result tents disappeared; one of the last was Codona's cinema tent in Leith's Parliament Street which in 1912 was replaced by an iron shed seating two hundred and bearing the name The Magnet, Coalhill.

Better accommodation inspired an expectation of better films, and these gradually appeared. An average picture show would total three or four dramas interspersed with interest films, and would run for up to ninety minutes. Before 1910 there were six main outlets for films in Edinburgh — the West End Theatre in Shandwick Place, Pringle's Grove Street and Elm Row, Cinema House at Surgeon's Hall, Queen's Hall in Queen Street, and the Operetta House. The entrepreneurs running them, and smaller houses in the capital and its port of Leith, tended to fall into two categories. Some were showmen taking a step up from their fairgrounds, while others were financiers investing in a burgeoning form of public entertainment. This latter category included corporate organisations which came on the scene before the First World War.

J.J. Bennell's films were shown at both the Operetta House and at the West End. His organisation had as one of its aims the spreading of the Christian message, and the jingle sung by child patrons at their matinees had a certain evangelical tone as well as ramming home an easily-memorised advertisement:

"BB pictures, they're all right,
always beautiful and bright,
I will sing with all my might,
go and see them every night".

Other cinema owners were less idealistic. Pringle, newly settled in two houses, had been a variety artiste based in Huddersfield. R.C. Buchanan was a former elocution teacher and actor who would later own the Palladium, Coliseum, and Princes cinemas and aspired to be chairman of the Scottish branch of the Cinematograph Exhibitors' Association and a Fellow of the Royal Society of Literature. The Poole family's entertainment always carried a high educational value, while Tindle was a technician and former bird mimic who succeeded Bennell at Shandwick Place. Other trade names in Edinburgh included Albin, a former musician, and Nicol Pentland, an actor, and to round off this very mixed bunch there was none other than "Captain Texas", who brought the fairground spirit into his Imperial Picture House in Leith by regularly shooting a clay pipe or cigarette from his daughter's lips, to the delight of patrons.

The second group of cinema owners were the financiers, most of whom entered the trade after the 1909 Act became effective. They included F.R. Graham-Yooll who was a scrap metal and machinery dealer probably connected with a Leith company of oil manufacturers and builders' merchants. From such a base he branched into the world of entertainment, becoming the builder of the Gaiety in Leith and owner of the Marine Gardens, Portobello. F. Lumley was the owner of the Powderhall racing track, as befitted a supplier of athletic equipment, and he entered the cinema world through building roller-skating rinks. His partner was J. Maguire, a bookie who mixed his racing interests with shipbuilding and a directorship of the King's Theatre. These three names recur again and again in the story of the capital's cinemas — in particular we have to thank the unlikely combination of Lumley and Maguire for the Playhouse.

The great cinema chains were beginning to grow at about this time. Provincial Cinematograph Cinemas opened two houses in Princes Street before the First World War with the avowed purpose of placing "a refined form of entertainment" before the public. In fact the opening of their Picture House in Princes Street on July 20th 1910 was defined by Roderick Ross, Chief Constable, as the first proper cinema opening in the city, and began a spate of "respectable" picture houses. These tended to be small by later standards but had refinements — Cinema House, Leith, had potted palms. Ten cinemas opened in the city in 1913 and four more in the pre-war months of 1914.

The war to end all wars had a number of serious effects on the British film industry. It brought closure to a quarter of the nation's cinemas, usually single-owner houses like the Imperial in Leith's Kirkgate or the Waverley in Infirmary Street, Edinburgh. This was partly due to the diverting of celluloid into armaments production and the calling up of male cinema staff. The conflict had other long-term effects too — it allowed the American film industry to establish a base in the British market, to the near-exclusion of the native product in our own times. It also forced the industry to live with the idea of being a largely working-class phenomenon. After the war, cinemas were large palaces decorated in confused taste, in place of earlier, intimate, almost tasteful cinemas. All classes appear to have visited the cinema, but the working-class went more frequently.

Too big a market to be dominated by middle-class standards of taste, the pictures took working people out of the pubs and broadened their horizons. This earned some qualified praise from Edinburgh's Chief Constable, Roderick Ross, who said in evidence to the National Council for Public Morals in 1917:

"It is the custom in picture houses in the poorer quarter of the city for a considerable number of women with children in arms to attend these places late at night. In one picture house in one evening after 8 p.m. no less than forty-two women with children in arms were seen to leave the premises. This is a matter to be deplored, but it is no doubt due to the fact that most of the husbands of these women are at present on active service with H.M. Forces and no doubt these women are glad to have a little relaxation from the weary round which is theirs".

Ross declared that there were twenty-four picture houses in Edinburgh in 1917 (Leith was still then a separate burgh), seating 17,000; in other words one seat for almost every twenty inhabitants. But the "numbers game" for early cinemas is dangerous, not only because of the unreliability of early statistic-gathering, but because of the overlap between theatre, cinema, and public hall. At the lowest end of the market a cinema was a box with auditorium, projection room, a piano, and lavatories; at the upper end it had tearooms and an orchestra. (The Palace cinema in Princes Street cost around £10,000 to build in 1913). Statistics become even more confusing because figures and addresses given in the *Kinematograph Year Books* are often outrageously wrong, for business reasons as well as clerical error. Working from these, historian Rachael Low reached a different ratio of cinema seats to population than did Ross. Her figures give one seat per fifteen people in Edinburgh in 1914, working on a total of thirty-eight cinemas.

In the poorer districts horrific stories are told of fleas — and worse. In the "Starry", St. Mary's Street, a local informant claims that a boy patron was not expected to leave his seat to relieve himself but did so against the row in front, being rewarded by a jet of disinfectant in his direction from the usher's syringe! Paying for entry with jam jars is a cinema legend, but one difficult to authenticate. The story of jam jar entry to the Star is probably untrue but was conceivably possible at the Waverley, Infirmary Street, closed in the First World War. Even after the war Leith's Gaiety is said to have issued red coupons for tickets in exchange for jars.

Chuckers-out were employed against drunks and prostitutes, and the latter's activities were a constant cause for concern to cinema managements and the police. No Edinburgh cinema showed its films in complete darkness.

1918-1939 : TALKIES AND SUPERCINEMAS

Between the wars the cinema boomed — but might have bust in 1929-30, when Wall Street crashed, had the Talkies not come along. It is a moot point whether silent films could have sustained enough public interest to justify the 1920s and 30s vogue for building huge palace-like picture-houses, despite the efforts of cinema proprietors to provide home-made music and sound effects.

The American style of the time was to "build big" in order to achieve economies of scale. Thus the Supercinema was born. It was after a visit to the USA that Maguire and Lumley opened the Playhouse Theatre, Greenside, influenced by such trans-Atlantic wonders as the New York Roxy. Its design had been influenced by the Scots-born American architect, W.R. Lambe, who used traditional architectural styles to achieve an effect of massive luxury. He ransacked the palaces of the past for any idea which could be turned into a cornice or a handrail.

Not surprisingly, the Playhouse was hailed by *Cinema Building* as Edinburgh's Roxy, for its size if not its style, offering as it did more than 3,000 seats. This was not the largest in Scotland, that honour going to Green's Playhouse (now the Apollo) in Glasgow, seating 4,400. However by the late Twenties the trend seemed to reverse towards smaller cinemas, the *Kinematograph Year Book* declaring that the ideal size was for buildings seating 1,500. Large houses, it said, could not operate profitably because there was too much competition. It is significant that no cinema bigger than the Playhouse was built in the capital and that Edinburgh's Supercinemas, like the New Tivoli, Regent, or Astoria, pivot round the figure of 1,500. The opening brochures for both the Tivoli and the Astoria explain:

"The Super Cinema has with some people the meaning, a building seating thousands, with everything in proportion, and to others it means THE BEST".

George   Kevin & Henry Wheelan

A very Edinburgh solution to the problem of expense!

In addition to Lambe, there were three other architectural influences on the city cinemas — Eberson, the Odeon package, and Art Deco. Eberson trade-marked the "Atmospheric" concept, best seen in the Majestic, Houston, in 1923. In its full glory an "atmospheric cinema" provided the audience with the illusion of open-air decor and a foreign theme. Pringle's Theatre in Elm Row was for a time known as the Atmospheric and bits of artificial greenery were found in the ceiling by Gateway staff long afterwards. The New Victoria's starlit ceiling and Grecian statues also reflect this theme and can still be seen, despite the present tripling arrangement at the Odeon.

The leading architect of Edinburgh cinemas was T. Bowhill Gibson, who had three city cinemas opening in 1930 alone — Astoria, Blue Halls, and Rutland — each in a different style. As the decade progressed he was increasingly drawn to the Odeon design of cinema — spare, modernist, brandishing an advertising tower guarded by unsleeping neon lights. Gibson's splendid County/George, Portobello, was built in the Odeon style in 1939, the last supercinema to be erected in Edinburgh. Unfortunately the building has since been "beheaded". (This Odeon style should not be confused with the Edinburgh cinema of the same name as this was originally the New Victoria.)

The third architectural influence was Art Deco, short for "Art Decoratif". In the inter-war period many of the capital's cinemas exhibited characteristics of the style and these can often still be recognised — octagons, sunray patterns, stylized flowers, a general bendiness, verticals and horizontals used like lines drawn on a wall. To find Art Deco, keep your eyes open for detail — like the splendid sand-blasted windows at the New Tivoli.

However the continuation and growth of the Supercinemas was only made possible by the arrival of Talkies which averted the major threats of the late Twenties — bankruptcy and a saturated market. As it was, there was no further cinema building in Edinburgh after 1939 except in unusual circumstances. Although the Second World War, and the years immediately after, brought peak audience figures, they ironically saw the decline in the rate of cinema building. When the Embassy opened in Pilton in 1937 it was said to be one of a chain of cinemas planned for such suburbs as Morningside, Gorgie, and Stockbridge, an ambitious scheme aborted by war.

Before Talkies arrived, exhibitors were painfully aware of the lack of sound. Home-made special effects were tried — klaxon horns, rattles for horses' hooves etc. J.R. Poole tried out a controlled explosion in a dustbin (disastrously) for *The Four Horsemen of the Apocalypse* at the Synod Hall. At one time ushers in Princes Street cinemas were cracking the ends of rows with canes to simulate pistol shots! Music came from pianos, trios (Palace, Savoy), and orchestras (St. Andrew's Square, Synod Hall). One Princes Street house had a trio playing selections from Verdi, Caffot and Lacalle. The standard of these orchestras was generally low, until Graham-Yooll introduced "Sam and his Orchestra" to the St. Andrew's and brought crowds to Clyde Street. Not to be outdone, Poole hired himself an orchestra leader from London too. Live musicians tended to disappear when cinema organs became fashionable, although at the Playhouse both organ and orchestra were used for a time. This cinema's organ, a Hilsdon from Glasgow, cost £15,000. With the advent of Talkies, the Caley gratefully cancelled its order for an organ, while the great Wurlitzer later ordered for the Embassy, Pilton, found itself at the New Victoria, which had Provincial Cinema money behind it.

Talkies are considered to have begun in 1927 but they had an interesting "prehistoric" period, in which Edinburgh figures. As early as 1902 Poole's Myriorama at the Synod Hall included singing pictures of Bertha Tilley, and eleven years later the Lyric in Nicolson Square was advertising the Kinetophone featuring the "Toreador" song from *Carmen*. On September 13th 1926 Poole showed an early Lee de Forest "phonofilm" to capacity audiences — with a banjo, guitar, and barking wolf being both seen and heard. These accompanied the silent Sir John Martin Harvey in *The Only Way*, and with this show Edinburgh seems to have been in advance of its English counterpart as the Leeds-based Forest films were not shown at London's Capitol until a fortnight later, during a vaudeville performance. Talking pictures continued at the Synod Hall and on October 26th 1926 the Castle Terrace audience saw Graham Moffat's company in the Scots comedy *Till the Bells do Ring*, also on de Forest "phonofilm".

What are now regarded as the first Talkies were born in 1927 when recording equipment in the musical *The Jazz Singer* picked up the words "Wait a minute — you ain't heard nothing yet". The first proper Talkie was Al Jolson's *The Singing Fool* with wax discs playing from the inside out, the opposite of modern records, to synchronise with the film — in theory.

The Singing Fool came to Edinburgh late, running at the New Picture House, Princes Street, for five weeks from June 10th 1929. There is some doubt about who was the chief operator responsible for showing this cinema innovation — Fred Mitchell who claimed the honour in 1949 or G. Thomson who made a similar claim in 1959. Either would have had to glue his eyes to the screen for up to 150 performances while the queues stretched to St. David's Street humming "Sunny boy" and "I'm sitting on top of the world". Said the *Evening News*:

> "There is no gainsaying the fact that the average cinema public are attracted by a film which can produce tears. There was a time when such a statement could have been rigorously denied".

The Edinburgh Talkie race was on. Poole's early "phonofilms" were quite forgotten, so on July 29th 1929 Poole's Synod Hall showed *Speakeasy*, a New York boxing and nightclub drama, using RCA apparatus. A contemporary reviewer thought this system superior to the New's but in the later opinion of J.K.S. Poole, the audience could barely make out ten words spoken in the entire film. The Synod Hall just pipped the

Alhambra in being second with sound, the latter starting to Talk on August 3rd. The Playhouse opened for the first time with a Talkie on August 12th, the Capitol and the Savoy were next by the twenty-seventh of the month, and were followed in September by the Lyceum, Ritz, and Salisbury. On October 15th Old Town residents were seeing sound films at the New Palace and on the 21st the "home of eloquent silence", the St. Andrew's Square cinema, broke the quiet of its backstreet with *King of the Khyber Rifles*. The Ritz opened equipped only for Talkies and was praised for its "bravery" in those days when film-makers and cinema-managers were still unsure whether Sound was here to stay.

However within a year almost every cinema in the capital was showing Talkies and only the audience kept comparatively quiet. All through the silent days they had talked and cheered!

Conversion to sound was essential for any first-class cinema as the Palace in Princes Street soon found out. Its accounts for the period between the end of November 1929 and October 1930 carry the dittoed remark "talkies doing the business". The Palace caught up with the rest on November 10th 1930 showing *Sunny Side Up*, although by this time wax discs had generally been replaced for sound reproduction by film soundtracks, an improvement pioneered by the Pathe News Bulletins. The sheer variety of sound equipment and the pace of technological improvement in cinema science made life increasingly difficult for cinema-managers trying to keep their audiences happy.

AFTER 1939 : FAILED HEROES

Cinema-going was one of the nation's favourite pastimes in the Thirties and audiences increased throughout the decade. Not only were films getting better — many of them still grace our television screens nowadays — but the cinemas themselves were becoming part of community life. Organs were still popular, both in their own right and for encouraging community singing. Some houses, like the New Tivoli, kept up variety programmes too.

Temporarily closed at the outbreak of the Second World War as an emergency measure — until Margot Asquith wrote to *The Times* suggesting their reopening to provide variety and relaxation — picture houses found the war years to be comparatively prosperous. A "plateau" of attendance figures was reached and did not begin to slope off until around 1948. In Edinburgh the Palace in Princes Street came into its own as a Sunday "garrison cinema", peaking at 571,529 attendances over 1942-43, while in 1945 it housed 15,000 people in a week to see *The Seventh Veil*, totalling 484,000 for that year.

Cinema also created the first mass youth market — for children as they were then called. The first children's film club in the city started at the New Tivoli in 1934. This was the Mickey Mouse Club which by 1938 had 5,000 members throughout Scotland. Matinees for youngsters had also been held in Poole's Synod Hall but when Poole's Roxy was opened the Mickey Mouse Club transferred to this new cinema along Gorgie Road. Sessions included safety-first films and quizzes, and a children's committee was appointed. GB Kiddies' Clubs were run by Gaumont-British at the Capitol in Leith and at the New Victoria, the latter beginning in 1941. The GB song went as follows:

"We come along on Saturday morning,
greeting everybody with a smile.
We come along on Saturday morning,
knowing it's well worthwhile.
As members of the GB Club, we all intend to be
good citizens when we grow up
and champions of the free.
We come along on Saturday morning
greeting everybody with a smile - smile - smile,
greeting everybody with a smile."

By 1947 the three city clubs had a combined membership of 4,000. An analysis by John Mackie of children's cinema-going habits in 1933 found that 69% of Edinburgh youngsters went to the cinema once a week, 19% twice weekly, but only 13% once a month. Boys went more frequently than girls and poorer children more frequently than their middle-class counterparts, with a quarter of working-class boys going to the pictures twice a week. On the other hand senior girls went less frequently as they grew older. These figures were confirmed by J.B. Barclay as applying in the Forties and Fifties but by 1961, while the number attending once weekly remained steady, many fewer went twice a week. However most schoolchildren expressed a preference for films over television. Had the cinemas received equal loyalty from their adult patrons, the decline in attendance figures might have been less steep. But for the cinemas as a whole, the way was down.

In 1946 there were 1,635 million admissions to cinemas throughout the UK; by 1955 this was down to 1,182 million. The cinemas countered with novelty and with bigger films. 3-D lasted a short time in the Fifties, but produced too many problems in the way of headaches and patrons "forgetting" to return their red and green-lensed spectacles. Interestingly, 3-D is again something of a cinema novelty in our own time but it has certainly never revolutionised picture-going as Talkies did. Publicity stunts were also a means of maintaining attention on the picture houses, and Edinburgh managers were not slow to

St. Andrew's Square Cinema   RCAHMS

publicise their product. For *Cleopatra* a lady member of the Odeon staff spent an afternoon in the foyer bathing in thirty gallons of milk. The same cinema held dog matinees to publicise *In the Doghouse* and *Savage Sam*, with ice-cream girls selling bones and biscuits. Of course all this was in the traditional showman's spirit — back in 1925 a Legionnaire had paraded in Princes Street (to the horror of the police) to promote *Beau Geste* at the Caley, and a camel went wild on the steps of the Usher Hall during the advertising of Poole's *Across the Sahara*.

1953 saw an accumulation of technical gimmickry to show the Coronation films *A Queen is Crowned, Elizabeth is Queen*, and *Coronation Day*. Special wide-screens were prepared at the Monseigneur (later the Jacey) and Poole's Roxy, while the latter cinema, along with the Cameo, had its loudspeakers cunningly arranged to create stereo effects : "as the aircraft fly over Buckingham Palace the sound passes overhead and passes away from us". Significantly however, the Coronation also gave people their first sight of a television screen, even if it was only in a shop window.

This was the beginning of the wide-screen era. In the mid-Fifties Twentieth Century Fox was about to issue *The Robe*, its first CinemaScope epic, insisting that all such films should be accompanied by stereo sound. Small cinemas found the expense of installing vast curved CinemaScope screens (often reducing seating capacity) too severe to consider re-equipping for stereo as well. The champion of the district cinemas' point of view was J.K.S. Poole who proved at his Roxy that sound reproduction for the new screens could be adequate without stereophony. However the Caley installed the system and won the prize — *The Robe* with Fox films guaranteed for two years. *The Robe* was the first of a wave of new screen epics and it is ironic that the cinema's years of decline also brought unprecedented long runs. The legendary triumph of *The Singing Fool* was eclipsed by the Playhouse showing *The Guns of Navarone*

for two months, *My Fair Lady* at the Regal for three, six months of *South Pacific* at the New Victoria, and longest of all, the run of eighteen months for *The Sound of Music* at the Odeon from 1965-67. (Although *Gregory's Girl* was shown in Dominion 3 from 1981-83, this was in a considerably smaller auditorium.)

Cinemas were already beginning to close and some historians see this as a result of increasing monopoly within the industry. Edinburgh may have helped start this national trend by providing an early base at the Haymarket cinema (later the Scotia) for John Maxwell, the Glasgow lawyer who built up the ABC chain. This comprised 304 halls at his death in 1940 and included the city's Regal and Ritz. Provincial Cinematographic Theatres established itself early in the capital at the Picture House, Princes Street, later joining with Gaumont-British (purchaser of the St. Andrew's Square cinema from local owner F.R. Graham-Yooll) in J. Arthur Rank's empire. With more cinemas duplicating each others' programmes the result was a reduction in the choice of films available to the selective cinema-goer.

Another major factor in the dropping of audience figures was "the cancer of the X film" which destroyed family audiences. However in view of the increasing sophistication of audiences it is difficult to imagine an alternative. Interestingly, the Dominion refused to show an X until the Seventies, and has survived.

There are doubtless other reasons for the plummeting of cinema audience statistics, which fell from 1,182 million in 1955 to 327 million in 1965, 103 million in 1977, only to plunge to double-figure millions in the Eighties. The Entertainment Tax could have been blamed for all this, but what about the 70% *ad valorem* duty on film prints, the spread of television, liberalisation of gambling laws which set bingo loose upon the public, and what of the upsurge of teenage delinquency and the vandalism often associated with it? In September 1959 the Lyceum cinema banned any would-be patron wearing jeans. "Unless you're close to this problem", the manager told the *Evening News*, "you can't appreciate what cinema managers have to go through." These three social innovations — the popularity of bingo and television and the rise of an independent youth culture — show that society has undergone a complete upheaval and cinemas can no longer expect to accommodate whole families, streets, or neighbourhoods.

Only two courses of action appear open to cinema managements nowadays. One is to convert to cinema complexes offering two or three programmes under a single roof. The ABC, Odeon, and (privately-owned) Dominion have all tripled, while Filmhouse in Lothian Road has two screens. The last-named is an example of the alternative future for cinemas — appealing to a specialist audience, in this case, to those who wish to see a cosmopolitan programme of films. Edinburgh has a long tradition in its appreciation of cinema as an art form beginning with its Film Guild as far back as 1929 and Filmhouse is the successor to the Guild's previous cinema in Randolph Crescent. In its own way perhaps the La Scala/Classic also fulfils the definition of a specialist cinema, with its "adult" films.

However, these recent developments do not foretell a return of cinema glories. Surviving cinema buildings, whether in use as cinemas or not, are clearer vestiges of that glory — mannered magnificence in the Caley, modernism in the George, Portobello, and classic but camp elegance at the Odeon. Cinema buildings come in a farrago of styles and their study can be an introduction to many schools of architecture — classical, Gothic, the variously "historical". Most closed cinemas, if not actually demolished, have become furniture showrooms, supermarkets, bingo halls and banqueting suites. Many have regrettably deteriorated due to the absence of working ventilation. But even a piece of pink plaster in a supermarket, a cornice or entablature on a shopfront, or a quirk of decoration in a club, indicates to the alert eye that there once passed this way a thousand fantastic films.

Picture House Kiosk

What follows in this book is an alphabetically-listed description of Edinburgh cinemas past and present. Those cinemas which had more than one name are listed under their best known title, with its alternatives cross-referenced. The book may not contain every cinema; for example there was a mystery picture house in Sighthill about which documentation is lacking. Sources in general are often incomplete, and where complete, are unreliable. But within these limitations this volume contains what information can be accumulated on Edinburgh's picture shows.

ABC FILM CENTRE *See* REGAL

ABBEY 30-32 North Richmond Street

The persecution of the Jews in Eastern Europe in the nine-
teenth century brought an influx of Jews into Edinburgh. Small
synagogues sprang up on the Southside, one of them at
30-32 North Richmond Street. When the Liberton Brae
synagogue opened, the North Richmond Street building became
a cinema.

The Abbey, or A-B as it was pronounced by the patrons (the
Operetta House nearby was the O-P) was entered by means of
an external iron staircase which is still well-remembered in the
area. The seats were wooden benches but unfortunately few
other facts are available about this cinema. It could have
opened in 1920 or 1921. Certainly it was managed by a Mrs.
Bertie, on behalf of Mr. James Stewart in 1922. Only one
advertisement was found by Baird, Edinburgh's first cinema
historian, and that was for August 6th 1921 — *The Painted Soul*
and *The Fatal Fortune.* The Abbey seems to have passed to the
Broadhurst family which opened the Rio, Craigmillar; but it
was certainly closed before 1933 — probably unable to rise to
the level of investment required for Talkies.

ALBERT HALL Shandwick Place

The Albert Institute of Fine Arts, which opened as a kind of
Victoria ,and Albert Museum for Edinburgh, was moribund
enough by 1882 to be advertised as premises suitable for wine
merchants. Its fortunes were various, serving as a theatre and
as a Methodist mission centre before turning into a cinema.

On September 28th 1908 the *Evening News* announced that
''BB Pictures'', a ''splendid animated picture show'', would be

showing nightly at 8 pm and twice on Saturdays for 6d (2½p) or 1/- (5p). BB Pictures (J.J. Bennell) was one of the most important early renters in Scotland, only to disappear with so many others with the advent of block-booking and other restrictive trade practices. BB Pictures had a strong publicity sense; its matinee jingle was:

"BB Pictures, they're all right,
Always beautiful and bright
I will sing with all my might,
Go and see them every night".

The exhibitors had a strong evangelical character, with their Glasgow house showing a Passion Play on Sundays. "Beautiful and bright" was also intended to remind the viewer of the visual superiority of cinema over its rivals the magic lantern and Kinetoscope.

The life of cinema in the Albert Hall was intermittent. On February 1st 1910, the *Evening News* heralded a grand re-opening — Tindle's Picture Concerts — which began with slides of a cup-tie at Tynecastle. Tindle was brother-in-law of Richard Thornton, partner in Moss Empires, and had formerly been a bird mimic, bioscope elocutionist, and a tour-manager for Harry Lauder before building up a small chain of cinemas based on Sunderland. He also devised a method for eliminating projection flicker.

There was another re-opening on October 9th 1913 featuring *Dr. Jekyll and Mr. Hyde* and *Wild Beasts at Large.* In 1915 the Albert Hall was called the West End Cinema but the proprietor was still listed in the *Kinematograph Year Book* (an unreliable source) as Tindle. By 1920 its owners were listed as the Scottish Entertainment Company, and its seating given as 900. This brought it within the range of cinemas for whom re-equipping for Talkies was a difficult financial strain. Its first sound film was *Mother's Boy* in 1930 (very much on *The Singing Fool* bandwagon) and its manager was Harold Davies, later manager of the Palace, Leith.

Closure came in the last week of January 1932 with Jack Holt

in *Vengeance* and Mickey Mouse in *Wild Waves.* Sunday evening concerts began soon after but finished within the year. The hall became the West End Cafe and has now been converted to private accommodation, but is still recognisable by the ornate decoration above the doorway.

ALHAMBRA 200-204 Leith Walk

The Alhambra, with its loggia front, was one of the most distinctive buildings in Leith, the work of Leith architect J.M. Johnston. The owners were a consortium headed by Henry Lees, Robert Sanders and James Baird, who had many entertainment interests in the area.

It opened as a Theatre of Varieties on December 26th 1914 with a concert in aid of the Belgian Relief Fund. Pictures were shown of the Front on the first night but they are believed to have been stills. When not looking at the stage, Leithers could feast their eyes on the barrel ceiling in panelled plaster with the flattened dome in enriched plaster, and when their eyes returned to the stage they saw Miss Nellie Bly. It is not recorded how many of them knew that there was a hand-operated pump draining the area under the stage. This was the spring in nearby Springfield Street and in the Thirties and Forties there were allegedly goldfish swimming there. The Alhambra also boasted the only two privately-owned street lamps in Edinburgh — the first mercury vapour lamps installed in the area.

The Alhambra became a cinema a few months after opening, although variety acts continued. Alf Beckett was appointed manager after his return from the First World War until the closure of the cinema on March 8th 1958. On this unhappy event Mr. Beckett bitterly blamed Entertainment Tax for causing a decline in cinema attendance figures. The last films were *Frontier Scout* (Tony Martin and Peggy Castle) and *Dance*

Alhambra

Kevin & Henry Wheelan

Astoria

Kevin & Henry Wheelan

with Me Henry. Permission to demolish was granted in 1960 but the demolition did not take place until 1974 — lasting a dramatic five weeks from January 9th to February 13th.

ALISON *See* LAURIE STREET CINEMA

ASTORIA Manse Road, Corstorphine

Opened on January 1st 1930 (like the Blue Halls, High Riggs), the Astoria was built for F.R. Graham-Yooll by T. Bowhill Gibson. The interior decor was particularly special: rose velvet curtains braided in gold with screen tabs of gold coloured silk gauze. Restful autumn colours were chosen for the auditorium, which seated 1,228. The Ingram organ contained twelve miles of electric wiring in its coupling system and could supply cathedral chimes, a harp, xylophone, drums and the like.

The Astoria kept its children's matinee until the bitter end, which came in 1974. The last Saturday children's show was *Anything for Laughs* and *Zeppelin,* with the last show of all on June 29th: *Magnum Force* (Clint Eastwood) and *You Don't Know Why You Came Here.* The cinema's owners, Kingsway Entertainments of Kirkcaldy, were refused permission to demolish and possible community uses of the building considered. However the site is now occupied by a supermarket.

ATMOSPHERIC CINEMA *See* PRINGLE'S PICTURE PALACE

BEVERLEY *See* BLUE HALLS

BLUE HALLS (BEVERLEY) 3 Lauriston Street

Occupying the site of a former cattle-market, the Blue Halls opened on New Year's Day 1930 as "Edinburgh's new talking and variety theatre". Its first film was *White Cargo,* shown in a 1,760 seated auditorium designed by T. Bowhill Gibson for F.R. Graham-Yooll. Another cinema opening on the same day with the same owner and architect was the Astoria, Corstorphine.

The Blue Halls closed on April 4th 1954 to the cries of Johnny Weissmuller in *Tarzan Triumphs,* supported by Rosa Clark in *Island of Monte Cristo.* The cinema reopened as the Beverley on April 26th 1954 with *The Robe* for which CinemaScope and stereophony had been specially installed. (*The Robe* had already been shown at the Caley). The cinema closed once and for all on November 28th 1959 with Rodgers and Hammerstein's *Carousel* and Gary Merrill and Nina Foch in *Yacht on the High Seas.* The building was later demolished and the Lord Darnley public house now occupies the site.

BROADWAY *See* PRINGLE'S PICTURE PALACE

BUNGALOW (VICTORY) 26 Bath Street, Portobello

As early as 1902 No. 26 Bath Street was described modestly as "a hall with lavatories". It is not clear when it became a cinema — in 1910-11 it was used for rollerskating and in 1914 Wilbur Harlan, an American who undoubtedly ran it as a cinema, made cinema-like alterations, including the building of a cupola and a front kiosk (architects G.M. Scott and A. Lorne Campbell).

The house later passed into the hands of the Forth Cinema Company, Glasgow, which owned it until closure.

In 1942 the cinema was renamed the Victory but closed on May 26th 1956 after showing *John and Julie* (Moira Lister and

Beverley

The Scotsman

Constance Cummings). The building was then used by James Scott of Portobello High Street for storing furniture and is at present a show-room for a bedding company.

CALEY 31 Lothian Road

The Caley opened on January 1st 1923 with G.B. Samuelson's *The Game of Life*. It seated 900 and its architects were J.S. Richardson and J.R. Mackay who created what was intended as a Renaissance exterior, including a Venetian arch and Mansard roof. The interior still glows with wood and luxury. It was enlarged in preparation for Talkies by McKissack, the Glasgow cinema architect, who increased the seating in the northern section to give a total capacity of 1,800, since reduced to 1,400. The proscenium arch has been covered. The Caley never installed an organ: it paid £500 not to take delivery of a Wurlitzer when Talkies began.

The cinema was built for R. McLaughlin (manager), J. Miller and others, who later built up a chain consisting of the Embassy (Pilton), State, Carlton, and cinemas in Kirkcaldy and elsewhere.

The Caley was the first Edinburgh cinema to combine stereophonic sound with CinemaScope — a condition imposed by the distributors of *The Robe* which was one of the Caley's greatest hits. Another post-war success was *The Prime of Miss Jean Brodie* which ran for six weeks. The cinema was for long host to private Sunday performances for the Edinburgh Film Guild, beginning with René Clair's *Le Million* in 1931. It was also associated with the Edinburgh International Film Festival before the opening of Filmhouse up Lothian Road, and the Caley's name was to be heard mispronounced on countless visitors' lips. However, like many district cinemas, the Caley — under new ownership from May 1984 — is now offering a mixed programme of films and pop music events, a venture deserving every possible support.

CALTON STUDIOS Calton Road.

Two years after the closure of the Grampian TV studios in Calton Road, the building became the Calton Studios, an entertainment and conference complex. The venture of Bill Landale and Steve Clark Hall, it provides food, drink, film-making facilities, and an auditorium seating 180. This cinema was opened in December 1977 with Woody Allen in *The Front* and was notable for giving an extended run to *Chariots of Fire* before it received Oscar recognition. Since the opening of Filmhouse in Lothian Road, films are only occasionally screened at the Calton.

CAMEO *See* KING'S CINEMA

CAPITOL Manderston Street, Leith

With seating for 2,300, the Capitol was the largest cinema in Edinburgh when it opened on September 21st 1928. In addition the new cinema had a large stage and a twelve-man orchestra. The architect, J.A. Ross of Wishaw, was evidently haunted by the great railway arch into which the cinema was fitted under the former Caledonian Railway's station intended for Leith Walk. Roman in its arched doorways and name, the Capitol is a miniature inauthentic dream of a Roman palace. Still visible is the impressive but rather short triple staircase (past the original entrance ticket offices), as are the now-empty seats of the balcony under the slightly domed panelled roof. Unfortunately the thematic curve of the pillared frontage has been squared off.

The Capitol was remarkable for music and a children's club. The resident organist was Lyndon Laird, who also drove a poster-bedecked lorry for advertising purposes. In the Forties, concerts were held in tandem with another Gaumont-British house, the Regent at Abbeymount, half the concert being given in the Capitol, half in the Regent. Boys and Girls' cinema shows started in the Capitol on Saturday mornings from 1944, each meeting opening with "Hi ya! Members — Hi ya! Bravo! Bravo!" The club had its own song (lyrics listed in the introduction). It was noted in 1947 — when the combined children's cinema clubs in Edinburgh totalled 4,000 members — that there were more non-film activities like talent contests, quizzes and singing in the GB Kiddies club at the Capitol, than in the rival Mickey Mouse Club at the Roxy.

The Capitol closed as a cinema on July 22nd 1961, after showing Stephen Boyd in *The Big Gamble* and Charlie Chaplin in *Days of Thrills and Laughter*. The children's club moved to the Regent and Rank opened the house as a bingo hall the same weekend. But cinema memories remained — in February 1979 a new organ was installed after many years without one. The reason? Leith people were still talking lovingly about the previous organ.

CARLTON Piershill

Designed by McKissack & Son of Glasgow (designers of the Lyric and the Tivoli, Edinburgh), the Carlton was built for the Edinburgh Cinema Properties Company, consisting of R.M. McLaughlin, W.H. Cameron and others. The 1,400 seater supercinema opened on December 23rd 1935 with Dick Powell in *Gold Diggers of 1935* and Josephine Hutchinson in *The Sacred Flame*.

The lack of suitable films and the comparatively small size of the auditorium were given as the reasons for the Carlton's closure, in July 1959. Its last advertisement was for Dale Robertson and Mary Murphy in *Sitting Bull* and Frank Silvera in *Killer's Kiss*. The building then became a lemonade factory and, later, a garage for a transport company, but no sign of the Carlton remains on the site opposite the opening of Piersfield Grove.

CENTRAL Casselbank Street, Leith (formerly Hope Street)

Unfortunately little is known about this cinema. Called the Central, it opened on December 2nd 1920 in a building which had housed Turkish Baths and had been run by J.W. Hodgson, "masseur and medical rubber". The first film programme featured the five-reel *A Man's Fight against Tremendous Odds* and part one of *Barabbas*. The cinema was listed as closed in the *Cinema Buyer's Directory* for 1936, but it could have stopped operating some years before. It seated around 500, making it not really viable as a Talkie cinema.

The building has been a Pentecostal Church since 1936, but is still one of the best preserved cinemas in Edinburgh. Behind the oriental facade it glitters with gilded ropes and bosses, while the seating is in perfect character (although it came from the Methodist Central Hall). The plaster screen has been effectively transformed into a kind of painted reredos behind the pulpit, and the windows, which have been let into the side wall since the cinema days, can on a good day give as magical an effect as any cinema lighting. The barrel vaulted ceiling has been lowered and the first-floor asbestos-lined projection room has been taken out.

CENTRAL (GEORGE) 281 High Street, Portobello

The New Picture House, Portobello, opened in 1915 but was known for much of its life as the Central. However on November 12th 1942 it was renamed the George after its new owner George Palmer of Glasgow and offered a combined programme with the Victory (formerly Bungalow); usually the sign of a cinema in trouble. One present-day Portobello shopkeeper remembers Mr. Palmer carrying his takings to the night-safe every evening (the streets were safer then) before catching a train homewards. When the County in nearby Bath

Carlton

Kevin & Henry Wheelan

Street was modernised in 1954, the name "George" moved to that wide-screen house and the High Street cinema reverted to being the Central.

The Central was noted for its tempestuous children's matinees where the diminutive patrons were often thrown out row by row, the more affluent of them promptly paying for re-entry. Despite such income, the Central last advertised on December 2nd 1961 — "This should be a good draw! *Dentist on the Job* (Bob Monkhouse) and *The Man in the Back Seat* (Derren Nesbitt)". The cinema was closing with a misprint, the leading film probably being *Dentist in the Chair*. For some time the building was a bingo hall (Bingorama) but is now occupied by Misty's Nite Spot.

CINE PLAYHOUSE *See* SPRINGVALLEY CINEMA

CINEMA HOUSE 18 Nicolson Street

Nearly opposite the Empire Palace Theatre where the first Lumière films were shown, there opened in 1903 the North British Electric Theatre, later known as the Cinema House. In 1911 it was following the American system of continuous performances from 2.30 to 10.30 p.m. and serving (such was the keen competition) free afternoon teas. During the First World War it became for a time "The Imperial" and was later part of the Gaumont circuit. Seating 500, it could not make the leap into Talkies, and closed on May 24th 1930 with *Sea Fury* (Mildred Harris) and *The Love of the Atlantic*. The Salvation Army Congress Hall at present on the site was opened in 1935.

Jennifer Neil, writing in the *Evening News* for October 25th 1949, said of the period before the First World War:

"But the memory I find most incredible is the fact that a child could go into the cinema (Cinema House) at two o'clock on Saturday afternoon, see a 3½-hour programme (firmly ignoring the screened appeal: 'All patrons who have witnessed the entire programme are earnestly requested to vacate their seats in favour of those standing'), be served with a cup of tea and two biscuits on a daintily set tray brought by an attendant and stay until it was time to go home to bed at eight or nine o'clock — all for the sum of three-pence inclusive".

CINEMA HOUSE (EMPIRE) Tolbooth Wynd/Henderson Street, Leith

This cinema welcomed its first patrons to an entrance hall graced with potted palms. Naturally it was described as "The Cosy House" at its opening on April 14th 1913 — a late example of the vogue for small select cinemas that came in after the Cinematograph Act. The first night audience saw *A Tale of Two Cities* and *For the King* in an auditorium seating 600 and managed by James Yuill for the Leith Photo Playhouse Company. However the valuation records for the following year show William Codona of Portobello — probably the proprietor of the Magnet nearby — renting the Tolbooth Wynd house and it appears to have been empty for at least part of the First World War.

It re-opened at Hogmanay 1917 as the Empire Picture Palace featuring Charlie Chaplin in continuous performances of *Tillie's Punctured Romance*. Owned by James Baird of the Alhambra syndicate and opened by James Muirhead ("Scotch Jimmy"), a former burglar who lectured on his prison experiences, the cinema's history is difficult to chronicle, with few entries for it appearing in the Post Office Directories. By the time Talkies arrived the Empire was being run by Ronald G.S. Murray but it vanished once and for all around 1930, probably too small to justify investment in sound equipment. The building, vacant at the time of writing, is still to be seen at the corner of Tolbooth Wynd and Henderson Street, a few yards from the Water of Leith.

CLASSIC *See* LA SCALA

COLISEUM 125 West Fountainbridge

At its opening on December 14th 1911 by Sir Robert Cranston, the Coliseum was the largest cinema in the capital. It had been converted from a skating rink by R.C. Buchanan and contained space for 1,800 seats. After the First World War it became the New Coliseum, run jointly with the Palais de Danse, and acquired a supper room and screen, a carriage porch and other refinements. By 1937 it had fallen into the hands of that snapper-up of Edinburgh cinemas, P.S.L. Lucas. Five years later it closed, the last advertisement being for December 28th 1942: Jack Oakie in *Navy Blues* and *Adventure in the Sahara*.

The Coliseum auditorium is now the foyer of the Mecca Social Club, Fountainbridge. The arch which was a distinctive feature of the cinema-ballroom has been removed.

COUNTY (Craigmillar) *See* RIO

COUNTY (GEORGE) 14 Bath Street, Portobello

This site was once occupied by a variety hall belonging to the well-known artiste Andre Letta. The hall was demolished and a cinema erected in its place by Henry Paulo and Robert Scott, opening on March 30th 1939 with *Snow White and the Seven Dwarfs* and *Air Devils*.

The present building is the most widely-known work of the firm of T. Bowhill Gibson, architects of so many Edinburgh supercinemas, and in fact the County was the last supercinema to be built in the city. It was also the last word in "mood engineering". The lighting was controlled by panels fitted to each projector, the panels all consisting of twelve self-cancelling keys labelled "romance, tragedy, comedy" and so on. This gave a fascinating succession of light conditions in which to view the curtains with their goldfish motifs. The auditorium walls were notable for the Art Deco vertical and horizontal lines. Outside, a neon tube and a "cyclo-troughing" mechanism illuminated the central tower whose light changed colour constantly and was a vivid centrepiece of the town skyline at night. However the entrance hall maintained earlier, more substantial traditions of cinema luxury, featuring terrazzo tiles and walnut panels. The balcony lounge in rich red tartan may not have been to everyone's taste!

In 1954 the cinema was reconstructed by George Palmer and became the "George". It was intended as a Festival cinema, drawing (it was hoped) sophisticated crowds from the Edinburgh Festival. The George claimed to be the first cinema in East Scotland to combine widescreen with four-track stereo and as a result secured an early showing of *The Robe*. One of its owners, Mr. Scott, was rumoured to spend his summer days sunbathing on the roof, which has now unhappily been altered for the worse by the removal of the glass advertising tower. The building is now yet another of Portobello's bingo halls, having closed as a cinema on Saturday June 15th 1974 after showing Richard Roundtree in *Shaft in Africa* and Yul Brynner in *Catlow*.

DEAN PICTURE HOUSE *See* PAVILION

DOMINION Newbattle Terrace, Morningside

The Dominion opened on January 31st 1938 as one man's war effort. After his experiences in the 1914-18 war, Captain W.M. Cameron decided to concentrate his interests as a precaution against the war he saw coming. After selling off his stake in the Miller, McLaughlin, Albin group which owned the Lyceum (Slateford Road), the Caley and the Carlton, he decided to build his own cinema. He had attempted to build an earlier, now untraceable, picture house in Sighthill in the Twenties, but the Dominion was to be a very special cinema. Captain Cameron already had the stone — the first to be artificially produced in Scotland. This was Craighall Cast Stone, produced by one of his own manufacturing interests. His architect was none other than T. Bowhill Gibson.

Gibson built the structure round a steel frame stuffed with brick and pebble, faced with the aforementioned rose-coloured stone which has needed little cleaning since. Erected in only three months, the Dominion was one of the last and most characteristic Art Deco buildings in Edinburgh.

You enter by an oak door with sand-blasted, acid-etched glass panels resplendent with sunrays and Indian plumes. The auditorium is dominated by a panel spine giving a 'cash-register' effect in the centre of the ceiling. The panel reaches the middle of the auditorium in a strip of what was once a blaze of red, green, and gold. The magic screen itself was enveloped in silver curtains and on this sea of colour played the Walters lights, altering the character of the whole scene with every change of hue. "There was always something to look at", sighed the present owner, Mr. Derek Cameron. Naturally, such a wonderland opened with *Wee Willie Winkie.*

The Dominion has maintained a family approach to films and did not show an X film until the Seventies but combines this homely policy with the traditions of the Supercinema. The restaurant still flourishes, being the only one under cinema management in Edinburgh. There is also a gift shop. The cinema twinned on May 25th 1972, opened by Moira Shearer, with the public being offered *Cold Turkey* or *On a Clear Day You Can See Forever.* The twenty Pullman chairs advertised were in fact domestic armchairs, more comfortable than any cinema seat. The 1980 tripling was actually an expansion — the first independent video cinema snuggled into a vaulted ceiling in the reception area. The Dominion has consolidated its pre-eminent position in the Edinburgh entertainment scene and can face the future with confidence.

EASTWAY *See* PICTUREDROME

EDINBURGH FILM GUILD

"Sick of Hollywood". That was the *Scotsman's* comment on the "raison d'etre" of the Edinburgh Film Guild, when reporting on the Guild's first annual meeting on October 27th 1930. The EFG had been formed the previous year to promote serious interest in cinema and was one of the world's first societies of its kind. In its first season it sponsored showings of "serious" films in commercial cinemas, despite something of a setback in its first show, when an audience containing ordinary patrons catcalled during Cavalcanti's *Rien que les Heures* at the Salon. However the EFG began private members' screenings of such classic films as *The Cabinet of Dr. Caligari* at the Ritz and *Le Million* at the Caley. The Guild can claim to have been instrumental in the setting up of the Scottish Film Council and the Edinburgh International Film Festival, the latter specialising at first in documentaries. By 1946 the EFG boasted 2,000 members — numbers possibly swollen by ordinary cinema-goers wishing to see films on (otherwise barren) Sunday evenings — so the Guild acquired its own cinema. Acting with a commercial photographic company the Guild moved into premises at 6-8 Hill Street, utilising a small cinema there until moving to Randolph Crescent in 1958. Nowadays the group has

Embassy

some accommodation rights in the Filmhouse and is still going strong.

Edinburgh's lesser-known cinemas

Some mysterious cinema entries in the *Kinematograph Year Books* can surely be discounted — like the Royal Electric Theatre, Royal Hotel Buildings, which is probably the New Picture House, built in the Mount Royal Hotel banqueting suite; or Lumley's New Cinema, presumably the Palace, also in Princes Street. Others can be ignored because they were only intermittently and never primarily cinemas, like the Methodist Central Halls, Tollcross, which had a long tradition of showing films. There were other likely cinemas about which little is known. These include the People's Theatre, 17 or 19 Blackfriars Street, the Palladium in Raeburn Place with the Strand almost opposite, and the un-named picture house erected by Captain Cameron at Sighthill about 1923. Films were also shown in standard theatres such as the Royal in Broughton Street and the King's. The names of cinemas varied, especially in the early days, between "Picture House, Picture Theatre, Electric Palace", etc., and by dropping or assuming the word "New" (as at the Tivoli) at the management's fancy.

EMBASSY Boswall Parkway

The Embassy was designed by James Miller for the Miller, McLaughlin consortium and opened on August 2nd 1937 with Myrna Loy, Spencer Tracy, Jean Harlow and William Powell in *Libelled Lady*. This was one of a series of luxury suburban cinemas planned for such districts as Morningside, Gorgie, Stockbridge, and even for the site of the Union Canal basin. The onset of the Second World War put paid to this ambitious scheme.

The Embassy had an eventful life, one of the highpoints being the visit of Yehudi Menuhin to give a recital for Edinburgh schoolchildren. After the auditorium had been damaged by a seat fire on Monday March 2nd 1964, the management called it a day, tired of battling against the vandalism to which the cinema was subject. Following closure, application was made for the cinema to be used as a dance hall or bingo hall but this was refused and the building demolished in 1975. A supermarket now stands on the site. The last picture show was *Day of the Triffids* (Howard Keel and Nicole Maurey) and *The Legion's Last Patrol*.

EMPIRE (Leith) *See* CINEMA HOUSE (EMPIRE)

EVANS PICTURE HOUSE *See* SPRINGVALLEY CINEMA

FILMHOUSE Lothian Road

Heir to the long tradition of the Edinburgh Film Guild, the Filmhouse in Lothian Road was funded in part by the sale of the Guild's Randolph Crescent premises. As a result the Guild has certain accommodation rights in the Filmhouse. The movement to establish a national film theatre in Edinburgh probably goes back to the foundation of the Edinburgh International Film Festival by the Guild in 1947, but it gathered strength in the general Seventies trend towards establishing regional film theatres.

A new company, Filmhouse Ltd., was set up in 1975. It bought St. Thomas's church, Lothian Road, and had it redesigned as a cinema by Ron Jamieson of Dodd, Jamieson. Cinema 2 opened in August 1978 with a temporary entrance in Morrison Street, and the main doors opened on February 15th 1982 when Cinema 1 showed Bertolucci's *The Tragedy of a Ridiculous Man*.

The Filmhouse is one of the best equipped cinemas in the country, with academy ratio, provision for silent speed films, stereo etc., but it cannot show nitrate films. To show these early films an explosives licence is required.

GAIETY (Chambers Street) *See* OPERETTA HOUSE

GAIETY Kirkgate, Leith

Leith's Gaiety Theatre appears to have adopted films as its staple entertainment diet just before the First World War. However, the site in the Kirkgate had a long tradition as part of the port's entertainment scene. The original theatre building was converted from a church and leased to H.E. Moss of Moss Empires. This company saved on costs by sharing variety acts between the Empire in Nicolson Street and the Gaiety, ferrying the artistes down Leith Walk in cabs after their appearances in the Nicolson Street theatre.

In April 1888, according to Leith historian J.S. Marshall, the church was damaged by fire and later rebuilt as a theatre by F.R. Graham-Yooll. Whereupon Moss leased it, renamed the Princess Theatre, and provided mainly variety shows in the 1,000 seater auditorium, although a Chalmers cinematograph was an early film show. This purported to show events in the Transvaal war, but was in fact shot in Wales!

By 1913 the Kirkgate theatre had been renamed the Gaiety and enlarged with a gallery, pit, and circle, with a shop on either side of the entrance. Films appear to have reigned supreme for about thirty years, but on July 3rd 1944 variety returned with Will Fyffe. The last picture show is not known but the last theatre production appears to have been *Laugh of a Lifetime* featuring Tommy Loman, Johnny Beattie, and the Four Kordites, in 1956. The Gaiety has now vanished, as has the old Kirkgate itself.

GAUMONT *See* RUTLAND

GEORGE *See* COUNTY (Portobello) *and* CENTRAL (Portobello)

GRAND 99 St. Stephen's Street, Stockbridge

Like many older cinemas the Grand had its roots in the skating craze, the site being a skating rink and ice store in 1895. By 1901 the Tivoli Music Hall had opened here, rising within three years to the dignity of becoming the Grand Theatre, with *Cinderella* as its opening show. Films were also shown but from 1909 the building became the Edinburgh Horse Repository and Riding Academy which had moved from Northumberland Street. There was said to be a retractable roof.

The Grand opened as a full-time cinema at Hogmanay 1920. It later was absorbed by the circuit owned by George Taylor of Glasgow and then became part of George Green's organisation. There was no balcony and its entrance from St. Stephen's Street was at the opposite end of the curved building from the present restaurant entrance. The last advertisement was on May 20th 1960, offering Olivia de Havilland and Dirk Bogarde in *Libel* and *Mission of Danger* in Metroscope. Closure followed four days later and this large building has since been put to multiple uses. Part is still garaging and furniture storage. The street-level floor has been a bingo hall and ballroom and is now a restaurant — Mecca's "Cinderella's Rockerfella's".

HAYMARKET (SCOTIA) 90 Dalry Road

Designed by A.L. Goodwin, one of the earliest cinema architects in the city, the Haymarket was sited in Dalry Road between a Post Office yard and a side street. The cinema entrance, an intriguing circular chamber, was placed crossways to the auditorium. A typical "bijou" cinema, the Haymarket seated only 675 people but amazingly survived more than fifty years after opening on December 13th 1912.

In 1946 the Haymarket became the Scotia, reopening with David Niven as *Bonnie Prince Charlie* on September 1st of that year. Its final picture show was presented on February 29th 1964 with John Wayne and Maureen O'Hara in *The Wings of Eagles,* supported by Stewart Granger and Rhonda Fleming in *Gun Glory.* The building is now derelict but the fine front of the arch can still be seen.

An interesting footnote about this cinema's history concerns its possible ownership by John Maxwell. It is believed that Maxwell took over the Haymarket, around the time of the First World War, expecting to sell it but instead found it profitable to manage. From Dalry Road he went on to set up a nationwide chain of cinemas which became ABC.

IMPERIAL CINEMA *See* CINEMA HOUSE (Nicolson Street)

IMPERIAL PICTURE HOUSE Storries Alley, Leith

The Imperial Electric Theatre opened on April 22nd 1911 but by May 15th was calling itself the Imperial Picture House. It gave two shows a night, and the manager, a Buffalo-Bill look-alike, was nicknamed "Captain Texas". He would shoot a cigarette or clay-pipe from his daughter's lips as a variety act, so Heaven knows what he did to the patrons! Further information about this corner of the Wild West in Leith would be welcome.

JACEY *See* PRINCES CINEMA

KING'S CINEMA (CAMEO) 38 Home Street

The King's Cinema opened on January 8th 1914, after unforeseen delays. The site's previous user is rumoured to have been a riding school although the Post Office Directories show a draper's establishment occupying this number in Home Street for several decades. The new cinema got off to a stylish start. It had the only mirrored screen in Scotland and its musical accompaniment must have been spectacular, being supplied by Madame Egger's Ladies Costume Orchestra. But it lived a quiet life until April 28th 1930 when Lady Margaret Sackville opened its first Talkie programme (*Married in Hollywood* and *Dance away the Night*) with Western Electric apparatus being used. Edinburgh District Cinema Theatres Ltd. later sold the cinema to a former manager of an Aberdeen filmhouse and it then passed in a neglected condition to the Poole family. At that time secondary lighting was still by gas and during inclement weather the doorman placed trays under the known leaks in the auditorium ceiling.

A transformation occurred on March 25th 1949 when Provost Andrew Murray opened J.K.S. Poole's new Cameo which showed *Le Paradis* and *La Symphonie Pastorale* in its first week. To its surprise Tollcross had a specialist continental cinema.

The idea for this can be traced back to J.K.S. Poole's wartime experiences as Films Officer for forces in the Middle East, when he administered mobile cinemas under the auspices of ENSA. In Jerusalem in 1941 he showed a Gary Cooper film with subtitles in French, Hebrew, Arabic, and German. Mr. Poole's enthusiasm for foreign cinema was further increased by his discovery of such classics as *Battleship Potemkin* and *Peter the Great,* amongst others, when in Cairo. Edinburgh audiences were to benefit from his cosmopolitan taste.

The Cameo kept up with the times. For the Fox Movietone *Coronation Day* in 1953 it devised its unique 'Audiophone', an

Cameo

Kevin & Henry Wheelan

arrangement of three loudspeakers which could simulate the noise of an aeroplane salute passing over Buckingham Palace. The Cameo also introduced a Milk Bar and received the first cinema drinks licence in the city on October 15th 1963. Gradually, there was less emphasis on continental films. As British films became less coy and generally better made, the Cameo's last decade was largely Anglo-American. *Tom Jones* and Woody Allen enjoyed long runs in a cinema whose absence since 1982 has made the capital a poorer place. The last picture show was on Saturday September 11th — featuring Gene Wilder in *Stir Crazy* and Brooke Shields in *The Blue Lagoon.*

LAURIE STREET CINEMA 6 Laurie Street, Leith

This Leith cinema opened on May 27th 1911, occupying the site of James Dick & Sons, grocers, where the Woolworths goods entrance now stands. The owner was the so-called Alhambra syndicate, and the manager was Willie Salvona, who remembered the showing of the first film in the Edinburgh area so many years before. Mr. Salvona came from a family of acrobats and this form of entertainment featured in the Christmas show at the new cinema. One of the later owners was Joseph Penn, who also leased the New Palace in the Royal Mile. Penn installed the BA sound system at Laurie's, reducing the seating to an almost unremunerative 470.

Officially the cinema was known as the Laurie in 1911-12; the Leith Picture House 1912-31; the Laurie Picture House 1931-34; the Leith Picture House again from 1934-44 and the Alison from 1944. Unofficially, less complimentary Leithers called it "the fleabox". The last advertisement was for October 7th 1946, announcing John Wayne and Betty Field in *Shepherd of the Hills* and *Power Dive* with Richard Arlen.

LYCEUM Slateford Road

One of the earliest supercinemas in Edinburgh, the Lyceum was owned by W.H. Cameron, R. McLaughlin and others, and was opened by Lord Provost Alex Stevenson on November 8th 1926. The new cinema was sited at the south-west corner of Robertson Avenue, where its architect Charles Mitchell raised a high dominating facade. The opening, featuring *The Greater Glory* and *Too Much Wife,* was an occasion of some grandeur, but the cinema did not have a particularly happy history, especially after the war. By September 1959 the manager had banned any would-be patron wearing jeans, and closure followed soon after, the last picture show being *No Kidding* (Leslie Phillips) with *The Man who was Nobody.*

As a bingo hall, the former Lyceum cinema continued to be troubled by vandals, who probably caused two fires in 1963. Their cause was never ascertained but £25,000-worth of damage resulted. The Lyceum's owners, now ABC, sold the building which was then demolished. Its site is now occupied by the garage and showrooms of Leggate & Co.

LYRIC (SILVER CINEMA) 30 Nicolson Square

Nicolson Square acquired its Silver Cinema on September 15th 1913 with an opening show consisting of *The Rival Airmen, The Niagara Falls,* and a western. In December of the same year there was even an early kind of Talkie — Edison's Kinetophone — featuring Campanini singing the Toreador song from *Carmen.* The quality of the programme indicates that the cinema's owners, W.H. Baxter and others, were catering for the posher end of the Southside trade at that time. On August 14th 1914 the cinema was renamed the Lyric, pronounced in the area as "Lie-rick" and did good business as a middle-sized house. By the end of 1929 it was in the hands of Alex Black, owner of the Picturedrome (Eastway), Easter Road. Talkies were shown for a while but Black's plans for alterations to the Lyric in 1934 do not appear to have been acted upon. Closure took place on March 28th 1931 with the last picture show being *Married in Haste* and Mabel Poulton in *Wildcat Hetty.*

The Lyric had a certain style. Its architect was the well-known cinema designer McKissack of Glasgow, who gave the cinema two bell-towers with cones, oriel windows wreathed in garlands and gleaming Carrara-ware fronting. If searching for the site of the Lyric in Nicolson Square, look for the Clydesdale Bank.

MAGNET Parliament Street, Leith

In 1912 Codona's film booth needed a new name. Formerly a tent, it was now housed in the luxury of an iron shed seating 200, so "The Magnet" was a not inappropriate winning title. Mr. Codona also had cinema interests at the Marine Gardens, Portobello, and in Prestonpans, and by 1915 appeared to be proprietor of the Cinema House round the corner in Tolbooth Wynd. Whether this implies the closure of the Magnet at that time is not recorded.

MONSEIGNEUR NEWS THEATRE *See* PRINCES CINEMA

NEW COLISEUM *See* COLISEUM

NEW ELECTRIC CINEMA *See* PETIT PARIS

New Palace   *The Scotsman*

NEW PALACE 18-22 High Street

This popular cinema was built in the High Street between Tweeddale Court and Fountain Close, opposite John Knox's House, by P.S.L. Lucas, a member of the well-known cinema-owning family in the city. Opening in 1929 with the Talkie *Her New Chauffeur,* and with seats priced from 4d (about 1½p) to 1/- (5p), the New Palace soon became a Southside favourite, queues often reaching to the bottom of St. Mary's Street. In 1936 the owner of the Laurie in Leith, Joseph Penn — who had married into the Lucas family — became lessee and was manager until his death in 1955. He left a memory of cigarettes and chocolates given as Christmas presents to regular patrons.

The cinema closed when the lease expired on September 22nd 1956, with the final films being *Captain Kidd* (Randolph Scott), *Smart Boys,* and *East Side Kids.* Recalling the last show for *Evening News* readers Bernard McGowan remembered that when the

"youthful audience tried singing 'Auld Lang Syne', the usherette cried 'Stop that racket! You're barred the lot of you. You'll no' get in next week!' "

The cinema had been too narrow for the installation of much up-to-date equipment; as it was, Todd-Ao had reduced seating capacity by a hundred down to 950. Not only that, but most of the Old Town community was on the move to the new housing estates in the suburbs. So the building became first a food hall and later, in the Swinging Sixties, McGoo's Club. It is currently derelict but the cinema frontage is still visible to the passer-by.

NEW PICTURE HOUSE *See* CENTRAL (Portobello)

NEW PICTURE HOUSE 56 Princes Street

Opened by Lady Piggott Redford on October 21st 1913, the New Picture House was intended by its builders to be a step up for the flicks. Provincial Cinematographic Theatres had a policy of building "refined" cinemas and they constructed the New out of the banqueting hall of the Mount Royal Hotel. An elaborate complex on several floors, the cinema could seat almost a thousand patrons. The marble was white in the entrance hall and green in the tearooms; one tearoom had a Wedgwood theme while the other was Louis Quatorze. Pannelled oak, tapestry, and coffered ceilings were extras and the air was guaranteed to change twelve times an hour. The architects were Atkinson and Alexander, of whom Robert Atkinson was to design the Regent, Brighton, eight years later, producing what is generally acknowledged as the first cinema of outstanding architectural importance to be built in Britain.

The opening show included a golf lesson on film from J.H. Taylor, Scottish Open champion, but the sporting highlight of the cinema's life was the 1922 Derby. The New, and its near-neighbour the Picture House, received film of the race by way of an aeroplane which flew direct from Epsom and dropped the film at the Marine Gardens, Portobello, the final stage of the journey being completed by motor-cycle. It all took seven hours. Other attractions at the New were a large orchestra and later the great cinema organ.

On June 10th 1929 the New scooped the first generally recognised Edinburgh Talkie — Al Jolson in *The Singing Fool.* It ran for five weeks, during which Edinburgh sobbed and queued as far as St. David's Street. This was not the city's first sound film (see the Introduction) but the days of the silent cinema were destined to end with Jolson. In *Coquette,* which replaced him at the New on July 29th, Mary Pickford lost her title of the world's sweetheart when she spoke on film for the first time.

The cinema closed as a Gaumont-British house on May 26th

New Picture House Tearoom   K. Wheelan collection

New Picture House Kiosk

New Picture House Foyer

New Picture House Auditorium

1951, with *Pagan Love Song* (Esther Williams and Howard Keel) and *Cause for Alarm* (Loretta Young). The New was sold in a block with the hotel and nearby shops to Allied Hotels, which retained only the hotel. As a result, where once was cinema is now Marks and Spencer's. The New had been blessed with long-serving staff. Miss Vaughan was cafe manageress for twenty-six years and Alex Ochiltree was foreman for only one year fewer. Lingering equally long is the memory of the downstairs Oak Cafe.

NEW TIVOLI (TIVOLI) Gorgie Road

Begbie's Farm Dairy provided the site for two Tivoli cinemas in succession, the first lasting from 1913 to 1933, the second opening in 1934. The earlier Tivoli was built by John Robertson, a member of the building family which erected the Caledonian Hotel, for a partnership also including R. Raymond and the Hearts wonder of the age, Bobby Walker. Opened on August 26th 1913, the Tivoli had an attractive traditional stage and showed touring variety artistes like Will Fyffe. The cinema appears to have been painted cream internally, had a high ceiling, with the projection box outside the auditorium, as required by the then-recent Cinematograph Act. At least part of the seating consisted of wooden benches.

Nevertheless the first Tivoli appears to have enjoyed a central role in local community life. It was the meeting place of the Old Hearts Association and was well placed for train and tram facilities. In the pre-Talkie days, when the music was supplied by a lady pianist, the audience made more noise than the films later did. Alistair James, writing long after in the *Evening News*, recalled a typical breakdown in projection:

"someone in the front forms now stands up and recognising a friend further back, calls 'Yoo-hoo' getting 'Yoo-hoo' back and much waving of arms besides. Others take up the cry and with a business-like look on his face down comes the chucker-out".

Although Filmophone came to the Tivoli, more drastic change was in the air and in June 1933 plans for demolition and rebuilding were accepted. James McKissack, of McKissack & Son (Glasgow), did the new house proud. The Art Deco stained glass, the balcony on its single pillar, the false columns with the cricket-bail beads; all these features can still be seen. The New Tivoli seated 1,999 and had a stage and dressing room for six artistes. It opened on January 1st 1934 with Buster Crabbe in *King of the Jungle*. Linked with Metro-Goldwyn-Mayer, the cinema could boast the first wide-range BTH Talkie equipment in the city and "mood" house lighting controlled by the projectionist, one of whom later remembered that "for Dracula, it was always dark blue". Mickey Mouse was an early resident, his children's club being based here from 1934 to about 1938 before moving along the road to Poole's Roxy.

The association of the Robertson family with the two Tivolis lasted until 1961 when Mrs. H. Wood (née Robertson) sold the house to GB Milne Theatres Ltd. and left in tears. Later Milne attempts to convert the cinema to bingo were opposed by a petition from 150 pupils from Dalry Primary but the end was only postponed and the last picture show featured Charlton Heston in *Planet of the Apes*, supported by *Escape from Planet of the Apes*, on July 28th 1973. After being operated by Kingsway Minor Bingo, the building is now a Ladbroke's Social Club, its sand-blasted windows still important relics of Art Deco.

NEW TOLLCROSS *See* TOLLCROSS

New Victoria   Harry North

NEW VICTORIA (ODEON) Nicolson Street

"The New Victoria is dedicated to those who
appreciate wholesome entertainment and who seek
to forget for a time cares of the workaday world".

So said the opening brochure of the Provincial Cinematographic Theatres' new venture. Seating 1,999, the "New Vic"
was opened on August 25th 1930 by Sir Samuel Chapman and it
dwarfed and outlived the many smaller cinemas nearby. At its
opening the patrons could be forgiven if their attention strayed
from watching Ralph Lynn and Tom Walls in *Rookery Nook* to
admire the new cinema's decor.

The auditorium was designed to represent a Greek amphitheatre, with a colonnade and statues (all female) round the
auditorium, Corinthian columns and a pediment for the screen.
The atmospheric starlit ceiling reinforces the concept of an
open-air amphitheatre, while the vestibule is a delight — a
curved delicate colonnade luring you round the bend to your
seat. All this was the work of W.E. Trent, an important
architect for Gaumont-British in the Thirties. A critic has
written of Trent's love "of the fan shape, the illusion of
Italianate palaces and open balustrades giving views of
Italianate gardens" — and related obsessions can be detected
in the architecture of the New Victoria.

The new cinema began its career with music provided by Sam
and his Orchestra, fresh from the St. Andrew's Square picture
house, but soon acquired a Wurlitzer organ. This came from
the Embassy, Pilton, which was glad to be rid of the unnecess-
ary expense when Talkies came in. This organ had the usual
"ready-mades" — siren, horses' hooves, motor horns, tele-
phones and doorbells, but was removed in 1964. It found refuge
in a company director's house in Fife and by 1977, the Lochgelly
Community Centre.

A description of the New Victoria's workings in the Thirties
reveals three large projectors, two spot lights, an operator's

lounge and a dressing room for six staff, thorough insulation for the rewinding room where spools were stored, forty fireproof compartments each having a spring door, a full stage with appropriate equipment, and a large monitor from which an operator controlled the house "rather like the bridge of a great ship with the captain in control". (*Scotsman Magazine.* September 23rd 1933).

The New Victoria later became a Rank cinema and was renamed the Odeon around 1965. Its history is dotted with premieres, stunts and charity performances. These include the appearance in the foyer of a Spitfire for the Scottish premiere of *The Battle of Britain,* a lady member of staff (Ms Dorothy Kent) taking a bath in thirty gallons of milk in the foyer to mark the opening of *Cleopatra* in 1964, two dog matinees and the 50th Birthday celebrations. The Odeon has also enjoyed the longest runs of the city's biggest cinemas — *The Sound of Music* from April 1965 to February 1967 and *South Pacific* which lasted for six months in 1958. A strong "live" tradition is maintained: Acker Bilk, the Dubliners, the Incredible String Band, were some late Sixties visitors, followed by Elvis Costello, The Hollies, Rush, and others in the late Seventies, when the stage was made three times as deep as previously, from December 13th 1978.

After 1941 a children's matinee club was run in the cinema. The Gaumont-British Kiddies Club closed (under another name) forty years later after showing the last episode of *Ambush at Devil's Gap.* Membership had dwindled to a few hundred children from all over the city.

An/American Werewolf in London was the last picture show at the Odeon before it closed for tripling on March 10th 1982. Happily, the rejuvenated cinema is once again in the forefront of capital entertainment.

NORTH BRITISH ELECTRIC THEATRE
See CINEMA HOUSE (Nicolson Street)

ODEON *See* NEW VICTORIA

OLYMPIA 54 Annandale Street

The Lumley and Maguire partnership built a roller-skating rink here during the Edwardian skating craze. Around 1909 Lumley was a seller of sports equipment and owner of the Powderhall track, while Maguire was a bookmaker and entrepreneur, but when roller-skating lost popularity they re-opened their rink as a cinema on February 5th 1912. It was vast for the time, with seating for 1,800. Two houses were given nightly, beginning with Wild West films. However the Olympia was probably too big to be profitable and by 1915 it was housing the Royal Italian Circus. It was later sold to Rossleigh's, the garage company, and the Standard Life Assurance Company now occupies the site opposite the LRT bus depot. Other schemes for a cinema in this street of exhibition halls came to nothing, including a scheme for an Odeon.

OPERETTA HOUSE 3 Chambers Street

This small house had a long record as an entertainment centre before it became a cinema. Carl Bernard set it up as an operetta house in 1875 but it soon degenerated into the Gaiety Music Hall and was the first step in the upward rise of Moss Empires. H.E. Moss tussled with hardened audiences here until he opened the Empire Palace, Nicolson Street, in 1892. Under the ownership of Lees and Sanders, the O - P as it was popularly called, began showing Edison's Animated Pictures in 1900 and by 1906 was specialising in cinema. Film programmes included such titles as *The Diamond Thieves* and *How the Poor*

Clown's Prayer was Answered.

Its life as a cinema was uneventful, its advertisements fitful and its entry into Talkies unannounced — probably as late as June 8th 1931. Closure took place early in the Second World War, December 23rd 1939 being the likely date. The building was by turns a furniture store and the National Health Insurance Centre until 1951 when it made way for Adam House. The latter building contains a plaque commemorating Sunday evening religious services which used to take place in the now-forgotten Operetta House.

PALACE 183 Constitution Street, Leith

Built by the Leith Public Hall and Property Company as part of the R.C. Buchanan chain, the Palace opened at the foot of Leith Walk on New Year's Day 1913 with *A Race for Inheritance*. Leithers, who were used to watching their films in tents, suddenly found that they had a (reputedly) 2,000 seat cinema which had cost between £15-20,000 to erect and was in the same class as the Princes Street houses. An interesting aspect of the building's design was the cantilevered balcony. The entrance hall is pillared and the touch of fantasy in the roof design immediately identifies the building as a former cinema. It is now a bingo hall, the final picture show taking place on Saturday December 31st 1966, featuring *The Trouble with Angels* with Rosalind Russell and Hayley Mills.

PALACE 15 Princes Street

Georgian in style, stone-fronted, expensively built — costing £9,000 said *Bioscope* magazine with bated breath — the Palace cinema opened on Christmas Eve 1913, although it was some months before the cafe and smoking rooms were ready for the public. The Palace was the work of local architect R.M. Cameron who also designed The Picture House further along Princes Street. According to the *Bioscope,* the hall was flanked "with heavy white Sicilian marble columns with decorated capitals", while the frontage consisted of "four fluted pilasters and a triple-light oriel window". On New Year's Day 1914 the new cinema showed a film of the Powderhall Sprint, the track there being owned by Mr. Lumley, who with G. Maguire, was owner of the Palace.

The new house prospered until it was hit by the arrival of the Talkies. From November 29th 1929 to October 1930 there is only one comment in the accounts — "Talkies doing the business", so the Palace's owners took steps to catch up with the new trend. On November 10th 1930 it reopened with the great Talkie success *Sunny Side Up.* However, the Palace had to fight for survival for some years, only coming into its own later. It often ran charity shows on Sundays and in wartime was a garrison-Sunday cinema. At the Palace you might have seen such historical dramas as *Disraeli, Queen Christina, The Scarlet Pimpernel* or a runaway success like *The Seventh Veil.* Shows were often held in tandem with the nearby Playhouse.

The Palace was a Princes Street landmark. Its Wedgwood Cafe, a popular late-night rendezvous, was reached through the wonder of a revolving door, and the doorman was the well-known Archie Poole (no relation to the cinema-owning family) who always wore his cap at a "Beatty angle". Despite somewhat cramped seating, the Palace was popular to the last.

A tempting offer closed the cinema, rather than a dwindling public. On February 5th 1955 the Palace showed *On the Waterfront* with Marlon Brando and *The Mating of Millie.* Then it closed without ceremony. The cinema had been bought by Woolworths whose store already stood next door and which expanded to swallow all trace of the picture house which so delighted the *Bioscope.*

Palace, Leith

PALACE (St. Bernard's Row) *See* SAVOY

PALLADIUM East Fountainbridge

Built as a circus by J.H. Cooke and opened on November 8th 1886, the Palladium gradually underwent a transition into a cinema by showing films from about 1908. Cooke projected these on to a screen hung from the middle of the circus, with those members of the audience behind the screen seeing the action the "wrong way round". However, the building opened as a cinema properly on February 11th 1911.

Its new owner was R.C. Buchanan, for many years chairman of the Cinematograph Exhibitors Association, and later owner of the Coliseum, Palace (Leith), and the Princes in the street of the same name. The Palladium was his first cinema venture in the capital and was later to be notable for being one of the very few city cinemas to install the Edibell Talkie system, its first sound film being *Voice of the City,* shown on March 17th 1930. The Palladium did not survive the difficult transition to sound and last advertised as a cinema on August 13th 1932 : *Mischief* and *Sky Spider.*

By December of that year the building was hosting Pinder's Royal Circus, although its future lay in theatre, with George Young, the Fountains Theatre Company, and Stagecraft Ltd. as trustees. It closed in 1966 to become a bingo hall but reopened as a theatre club when a licence was withdrawn. Eventually it became Valentine's Disco and is now derelict.

PAVILION 26 Dean Street

Around 1917 the Pavilion opened in a former church in Stockbridge's Dean Street, offering both cinema and stage entertainment. The first known advertisement was for March 17th 1917, offering Theda Bara in *The Kreutzer Sonata.* Seating 800, the cinema was run by the Alhambra syndicate led by Henry Lees. Tickets were priced from 3d to 9d (about 1½p to 4p), entitling the patrons to see variety turns which included, it is said, underwater knitting!

In the upheaval caused by the arrival of sound, the Pavilion was taken over by the Lucas family, who installed equipment for the projection of Talkies. So the cinema reopened as the Dean Picture House on May 12th 1930 with Jack Holt in *Submarine* and Audrey Ferris in *Beware of Bachelors.* However by 1936 the *Cinema Buyer's Guide* listed the Pavilion or Dean as closed. The building now consists of office accommodation and only the discovery of ceiling ventilation alerted architects to its previous use. For many years after closure it had been used for photographic processing and for the storage of tourist goods.

PETIT PARIS Shrubhill, Leith Walk

Situated about half-way down Leith Walk, the Petit Paris opened as the New Electric Cinema at Hogmanay 1908 with staff dressed in Napoleonic costume. It advertised eight performances a day for the showing of *Bluebeard,* and "New Electric" rock was given free to children at each matinee. Its date of closure is unknown — some sources suggest that closure took place before the 1909 Cinematograph Act became law, others claim that the cinema was destroyed by fire in 1912. The site was taken over by the Bass Rock Garage, demolished in 1962.

PICTUREDROME (EASTWAY) 12 Easter Road

Easter Road was able to boast its own cinema after the Picturedrome opened on September 2nd 1912. Within the year its seating capacity was enlarged to 600 and electric fans were installed. The cinema was owned by Alex Black, later the owner of the Lyric, but on his death the Picturedrome was taken over by Associated General Provincial Cinemas. This firm was run by George Palmer, more often associated with cinemas in Portobello.

On May 17th 1943 the cinema reopened as the Eastway, with Jeanette Macdonald and Nelson Eddy in *I Married an Angel* and Jack Buchanan in *The Middle Watch*. It was probably at this time that the house was enlarged to seat 875 patrons. Nevertheless, it closed on August 26th 1961 with an early evening performance of *Konga* (Michael Gough and Margot Johns) and *Hellfire Club* (Peter Cushing and Adrienne Corri). The building has since become a Cooper's Foodstore, but the shape of the cinema and its balcony can still be seen, together with some pink and white plaster.

PICTURE HOUSE 111 Princes Street

This was the first cinema to be built in Princes Street, where no fewer than four were situated at one time. The Picture House opened on July 20th 1910, a year before the cinema of the same name in London's Oxford Street, also part of the growing Provincial Cinematographic Theatre chain. This firm aimed to make cinema acceptable to a better class of patron — when opening their Norwich house they made this announcement: "The object … is … a refined form of entertainment, both interesting and instructive and entirely devoid of anything vulgar."

The Edinburgh house was designed by local architect R.M. Cameron and included a tearoom and a smokeroom. The frontage, with its flattened Corinthian tops to the would-be Grecian pillars and its Edwardian bathroom stained-glass in the kiosk, shows how cinema architects strove to capture a particular style while never quite getting things right. The decor was typical of the "gentrification" of the cinema in those years.

Eastway/Picturedrome

The Scotsman

The Picture House closed on November 24th 1923, with a showing of Brandon Tynan and Naomi Childers in *Success*. The early closure may have been the result of its small size (about 500 seats was usual in the early PCT houses) and the competition from other cinemas in the street, including the company's own New Picture House. The older Picture House was replaced by a Lotus and Delta shoeshop which in turn gave way to the present John Menzies store.

PLAYHOUSE Greenside

The building of the Playhouse was the most ambitious venture of the Edinburgh entrepreneurs, Maguire and Lumley. The latter announced at the opening of the cinema, on August 12th 1929, that he had planned a theatre for this site for many years. After visiting the USA the partners had been impressed by the economies possible in the palatial picture houses like the Roxy, New York, and on their return chose as their architect John Fairweather of Glasgow.

Fairweather used all the advantages of the site in constructing the Playhouse in three fireproof blocks. The building's design is classical with a central dome and rococo details in the auditorium. In the early years the stalls were dark crimson, the circle purple, and the balcony old gold, while extras included fifty dressing rooms, a tearoom and a soda fountain. The 3,040-seater cinema was the city's biggest and second in size in Scotland only to Green's Playhouse, Glasgow. It opened with a Talkie (these had come on the scene during the Playhouse's construction), the first film being *The Doctor's Secret*, based on a play with Scottish appeal, J.M. Barrie's *Half an Hour*. The next week it was followed by an Al Jolson-type film, *Weary River*.

A Hilsdon organ was installed although the orchestra was kept on for some time in the Thirties. However the organ was still a feature of the cinema even late into its life, the organist giving his appreciative audience a wave of the hand at the end of each recital as the organ assembly sank from view into the pit area. These audiences were unfortunately sparser in the Seventies as the Playhouse management found the seats harder to fill. The cost of twinning was considered to be too expensive and in 1973 the Playhouse was sold to a property investor. The last picture show in the capital's mightiest cinema was the James Bond vehicle *Live and Let Die* on November 24th 1973.

Happily, we do not have to record the demise of the Playhouse since that time. Its superb stage (74 x 37 feet) and auditorium attracted the attention of those opera-lovers tired of waiting for Edinburgh's new opera-house (for which another cinema was completely demolished — Poole's Synod Hall.) Thanks to the intervention of the Playhouse Society an orchestra pit has been added and the Playhouse remains part of the city's entertainment scene, hosting opera, pop and folk music, and, not least, films. Ownership passed to Lothian Region, and after a change in local government responsibilities in 1983, to the District Council which quickly sold it off to a private individual. A regrettable amount of controversy has surrounded these events but it should be remembered that not so long ago — in March 1974 — tenders for the Playhouse's demolition were invited by advertisement. Let us hope that the building's future is secure and long may its projectors whirr.

POOLE'S ROXY 430 Gorgie Road

The Poole family's answer to the increasing luxury expected of the Cinema was the Roxy, opened on December 20th 1937, with James Stewart in *Seventh Heaven* and Dick Foran in *Sunday Roundup*. Designed by Chadwick Watson and Company, the Yorkshire partnership which also designed the

Playhouse

Kevin & Henry Wheelan

Palace in Aberdeen, the new cinema had a hint of the galleon about it, with the main entrance where the stern should be.

The Roxy was at first treated with some suspicion by the locals, but soon won a place in their affections — probably through Mickey Mouse. Although the Roxy's was not the first Mickey Mouse Club in the capital (that honour must go to the Tivoli), the Roxy ran a vigorous club under the leadership of Chief Mouse J.K.S. Poole, sporting a Mickey Mouse emblem of office round his neck. The meetings began with the chant "Hi ya, members! — Hi ya, Roxy, Roxy!" The adults started to attend the cinema their children liked so much. Perhaps animals were lucky for the Roxy — its special relationship was with Twentieth Century Fox.

In 1953 the cinema acquired a wide screen, one of the first in Scotland. Its dimensions were 35 x 18 feet with a curvature of two feet, supposedly to give an illusion of depth, although the curvature was necessary because of the length of the new screens. However, Fox had very grand ideas about Cinema-Scope, for which wide screens were intended. CinemaScope, they said, needed stereophonic sound to go with it. J.K.S. Poole represented the majority of district cinemas in resisting Fox's demands because of the great expense involved. The Roxy sound system coped very well with the demands of CinemaScope without stereo equipment and with only minor alterations.

Built to catch the high tide of cinema success, the Roxy relied on twice-weekly patrons whose attendance fell away in the late Fifties and early Sixties. The last picture show took place on December 7th 1963 — Claire Bloom and Richard Johnson in *80,000 Suspects* and Rock Hudson in *This Earth is Mine*. From the ninth of the month the Roxy was run entirely as a bingo hall and Mr. Poole stopped his interim attempt at cine-bingo (a film and bingo session in one evening). Scotia Investments, then Coral Bingo, and now County Bingo, have run the house since.

POOLE'S SYNOD HALL Castle Terrace

The Synod Hall was a well-known Edinburgh landmark, facing across Castle Terrace to the Castle Rock. The Hall was the work of Sir Robert Gowans, the architect responsible for such distinguished buildings as the nearby tenements at 25-36 Castle Terrace and the fantasy pile of "Rockville", the unique private house demolished just off Colinton Road in 1966. In fact the Synod Hall was intended from the first to rival the European opera houses and was to contain a winter garden and an aquarium, but the complex actually built was less elaborate. It opened as the New Edinburgh Theatre on December 20th 1875, managed by R.H. Wyndham, but bankruptcy followed within two years.

The building acquired its name from being the Synod Hall of its next owners, the United Presbyterian Church which took it over in 1877 and altered it considerably. Bought eventually by the City Council, it was extensively let, containing for most of its life a bowling alley, rifle range, three dancing schools, the Royal Scottish Geographical Society, and many smaller organisations and businesses, along with what was to prove one of the capital's most popular cinemas.

There is no record of the first lease to J.R. Poole, who brought his family's travelling show to Edinburgh on December 22nd 1906. It consisted of a "Panorama, Diorama, Pauseorama, Marinorama, Militariarama, depicting scenes of world-wide interest, illustrating incidents which make the history of nations and continents". The Diorama was a form of illusory theatre consisting of an apparatus in which painted scenes were rolled from side to side like an ancient scroll opened horizontally. Three planes in depth, its frontal lighting touched the scenes with colour and magic. A lecturer gave a commentary and these often highly informative shows, with titles like *The Battle of Alexandria*, were interspersed with music and variety. The result so delighted Edinburgh audiences that it became a regular Christmas event at the Synod Hall, long after the Pooles had ceased to give Diorama seasons elsewhere in the country.

The Poole family were based in Gloucester but had cinema and theatre interests from Ipswich to Aberdeen. In the nineteen-twenties they lengthened their visits to Edinburgh and showed some of the great films of the day — *Covered Wagon* (1924), *The Niebelungs* (1925), and Valentino in *The Four Horsemen of the Apocalypse*. In 1928 the Diorama was shown for the last time and a new proscenium was installed. The Synod Hall was now a permanent cinema venue, despite a vain attempt by other cinema owners to impose a boycott. On September 13th 1926 the Pooles showed an early Talkie on Lee de Forest Phonofilm and in the following October a Talkie Scots comedy was exhibited — Graham Moffat's company in *Till the Bells do Ring*. However, Talkies arrived to stay at Castle Terrace on July 29th 1929, when *Speakeasy*, a New York boxing and nightclub drama, was seen and heard over £6,000-worth of sound equipment. In the opinion of the *Evening News*, it rendered "pure speech" with greater realism than previously possible.

The Thirties audience in the Synod Hall had a taste for action and adventure pictures but by the Fifties this had become a thirst for horror — "good, wholesome, creaking door entertainment", as J.K.S. Poole calls it. By now Synod Hall picture-going was firmly established in local folklore. Catcalls were usually heard during performances, while one patron often took a bugle to play from the audience if the show needed livening up. In fact the Hall was a manager's nightmare with no fewer than sixteen entrances, and side balconies arranged at right angles to the screen. The building's mazy corridors and general spookiness reinforced the Synod Hall cinema's claim to be the main Edinburgh centre for horror.

But some citizens still wanted an opera house and by the nineteen-sixties this was a recurring urban ambition. The first sign for J.K.S. Poole that the local council was seriously inter-

Poole's Synod Hall   *The Scotsman*

ested in the site for a possible development was the renewal of the cinema lease for six months at a time — an unsatisfactory way of running a business. With the acid note "This hall transferred to the Edinburgh ratepayers", Mr. Poole announced the last show for October 30th 1965 : Polanski's *Repulsion* and Macdonald Carey in *The Damned*.

The Synod Hall was demolished in the name of culture and has not been replaced.

Portobello : smaller cinemas

As a seaside pleasure resort, Portobello had a number of outlets for cinema shows, in addition to the Bungalow (Victory), Central, and County (George) cinemas already mentioned. One of these was the Marine Gardens which in July 1910 listed among its attractions a ballroom, concert hall, skating rink, and Hibbert's Pictures. The Empress Ballroom was the main attraction in this huge entertainment complex which stretched from King's Road westwards halfway to the present Cat and Dog Home site. It underwent many changes of function over the years, including barracks for troops in the First World War and a factory for the construction of amphibious landing craft in the Second. The area is now occupied by garages for both LRT and Eastern Scottish.

A cinema is believed to have existed in the Old Town Hall at 189 High Street, Portobello, and was known for a time as the Star Cinema. However in 1920, roughly twenty years after the town had been swallowed up by Edinburgh, the building became the Baptist Church and the picture shows ended. This site is understood to have been where the town's first resident, George Hamilton, built his house, which he named after the naval siege of Puerto Bello, in which he had served. Perhaps the adventure films pleased his ghost.

Research shows that the Tower Pavilion on Portobello Promenade was showing films in 1907. But as these were seasonal, little else is known about this early cinema. The Tower itself is still a feature of Portobello, incorporating relics from historical sites all over Edinburgh, and built to satisfy the eighteenth century taste for antiquities.

PRINCES (MONSEIGNEUR, JACEY) 131 Princes Street

The Princes Cinema was opened by R.C. Buchanan on September 14th 1912. It began operating on the then novel principle of continuous performance, showing a programme of westerns and an incident in the life of a dancer. Seating five to six hundred, it boasted a six-piece orchestra (likely to regale the patrons with Lacalle, Verdi, and Caffot), a tearoom and a smoking room. Less emphasis was placed on architectural features than in the other three Princes Street cinemas, although the manager had style. He was Nicol Pentland, born in Gloucester in 1883, and an actor in his own right.

In the middle Twenties the Princes passed into the hands of the Lucas family, owners of the Pavilion and New Palace, amongst others. However a decade later there was a touching closure notice, on November 4th 1935, advertising a complete Talkie set for sale. The last show at the Princes featured Jack Hulbert in *Love on Wheels*, Stan Holloway in *In Town Tonight*, and Mickey Mouse.

Remodelled for Scottish Associated News Theatres, part of the J. Davis circuit, the newly reopened cinema was christened the Monseigneur News Theatre. It always had a close relationship with Princes Street station nearby, relying on the latter to generate "passing through" clientele who had an hour or two to kill in the city centre. For showing the Coronation film it acquired a wide screen on June 8th 1953 but patrons complained that the new screen cut off the top and bottom of the frame. The Monseigneur was still a news theatre when it was

Poole's Synod Hall, foyer, 1962

Monseigneur (Princes/Jacey)   *The Scotsman*

bought by Jacey Cinemas and renamed the Jacey after some reconstruction in January 1964.

But the most remarkable change was still to come. When the closure of Princes Street station in September 1965 deprived the Jacey of its transient custom, it switched to full-length continental films shown three times daily. In the words of one of its managers it became "a specialist kinky film cinema", and distinguished itself by advertising Chabrol's sensitive film *Les Biches* as *The Bitches* although the original French word means a female deer! The restaurant remained but the Jacey finally received an offer too tempting to refuse and on May 3rd 1973 showed *Sands of the Kalahari* as its last matinee. The final picture show on the following day hit rock bottom: *I am Sexy* and *Do You Want to Remain a Virgin Forever?* So Princes Street lost its last cinema and a record shop occupies part of the site.

PRINGLE'S PICTURE PALACE (ATMOSPHERIC, BROADWAY, GATEWAY etc.) 41 Elm Row

The names given to this Leith Walk cinema over the years read like a history of twentieth-century entertainment — Pringle's Palace Roller Skating Rink, the Atmospheric, the Broadway and the Gateway, to name a few. But it was originally a veterinary college, run by a breakaway movement from the Dick Veterinary College in Clyde Street from around 1888 until its closure in 1904. A postmaster then stabled horses there and a printer ruled paper. The building opened as a cinema, and possibly also as a skating rink, on November 16th 1908.

The new proprietor was Ralph Pringle. Originally a variety artiste in Huddersfield, he became familiar with the techniques of cinema when touring with the Animatograph, a crude form of motion picture apparatus showing such films as *An Operation in a Dentist's Chair* and *An American Lynching Scene*. He seems

Pringle's/Atmospheric

to have been a member of the Biograph Company around 1900 and two years later gave his first film show in Scotland's capital, at the Synod Hall. Just before the Cinematograph Act became law he set up a chain of his own theatres — the Garrick in Grove Street, and the La Scala in Nicolson Street, as well as in other towns. There was usually a strong element of variety at Pringle's Elm Row, and this was emphasised in his advertising.

In 1929-30 the Elm Row cinema became known as the Atmospheric Theatre, with decor suggesting an open-air scene in a foreign clime (also seen at the Glasgow Toledo). Bits of greenery found in a sort of trellis roof in the auditorium as late as 1947 are vouched for by Miss Sadie Aitken of the Gateway Theatre and these were presumably relics of the Atmospheric. From February 23rd 1931 the house was called simply Pringle's Theatre and offered a roadshow. In 1932 it was Millicent Ward's Studio Theatre, in 1933 the Repertory Theatre, and two years later was the short-lived Festival Theatre. On November 28th 1938 it was renamed the Broadway and Mr. Alan Dale, later manager of the ABC Film Centre in Glasgow, remembers being sole projectionist in the wartime Broadway. Working there was a perilous business, since to get to the rewinding room he had to climb an iron spiral staircase, cross the roof and plunge down again into the building.

In 1946 the building and surrounding complex, including a billiard saloon, was presented to the Church of Scotland. Adopting the new name of The Gateway, the cinema/theatre opened in October of that year with seating for five hundred and a promenade cafe. The opening ceremony was carried out by Joseph Westwood, Secretary of State for Scotland, and the first public performance was of the films *Our Town* and *We of the West Riding*. But the Gateway soon developed a strong drama commitment with its own theatre company. It is not possible to establish the last films shown there as the 1965/66 autumn seasons were not open to the public, but Gateway members were in the habit of watching some of Cinema's classic films —

Brief Encounter, The Seventh Seal, The Red Balloon, amongst others.

The building is now STV's Edinburgh studios, but it is not so long ago that a "Roller Skating" sign was still visible in sand-blasted glass on the doorway of a building which has seen so many uses in the name of entertainment.

PRINGLE'S PICTURE PALACE (GARRICK) 71-75 Grove Street

This now-vanished building in Grove Street appears to have been a theatre for about ten years, under such titles as the Pavilion, Prince of Wales's, and Alhambra Theatre of Varieties, before films took over in 1906. As a cinema it is listed in Oakley's *Fifty Years at the Pictures* as one of the principal film outlets in that year. In fact Ralph Pringle did not open his picture house here until November 9th 1908, one week before opening his Picture Palace in Elm Row.

Little is known about this Grove Street house. Film shows are believed to have ceased in 1917 when Edinburgh Varieties converted it into the Garrick Theatre, and its most dramatic night occurred four years later. On June 4th 1921, after the evening performance, the vaudeville company stood watching its belongings burn, one of the company losing everything he had, none of it insured.

QUEEN'S HALL 5 Queen Street

This building, not to be confused with the present Queen's Hall in Clerk Street, was one of the earliest in Edinburgh to show films. Here T.J. West's Modern Marvel Company provided film programmes of a largely educational nature, in contrast to his competitors at the time, the Operetta House and the Albert Hall. On December 20th 1897 we know that the audience was entertained by an Analyticon — a device invented by John Anderson for projecting stereoscopic transparencies using twin projectors and a ten foot screen. Members of the audience hired for 6d (2½p) a small "analyst", not unlike 3-D spectacles supplied to later cinema audiences. Using these they saw church interiors and zoo animals. Later programmes included colour shots of London on a wet night and in 1905, as educational as ever, showed the work of a New Zealand meat factory.

Cinema shows appear to have been held at the Queen's until at least 1915. From 1924 the site became a schools' broadcasting studio, now converted to the studios of BBC Scotland.

REGAL (ABC FILM CENTRE) Lothian Road

The ABC chain of cinemas may have originated in Edinburgh where its founder, John Maxwell, is believed to have started his career with the Scotia in Dalry Road. Whether correct or not, it is undeniable that the Regal was the flagship of ABC's Edinburgh cinemas and, now renamed the ABC Film Centre, is still a major contributor to the capital's entertainment scene.

The Regal's architect was W.R. Glen, the leading ABC architect in the Midlands and the North before the Second World War. An exponent of Art Deco, he helped raise the standard of cinema design in the Thirties, his masterwork being considered to be the now-vanished Regal in Chesterfield. Edinburgh's Regal opened on the former Port Hopetoun canal basin on October 10th 1938. Its first show featured Charles Laughton and Elsa Lanchester in *Vessel of Wrath* and there was no cinema organ. The largest supercinema built in the city at the end of the Thirties, the Regal's size was eventually to its advantage, as it became the first Edinburgh house to triple.

The new complex was opened by Willie Ross, Secretary of State, on November 29th 1969. Cinema One was in red, showing *Goodbye Mr. Chips* (Peter O'Toole), Cinema Two in blue for *Ice Station Zebra* (Rock Hudson), and a bronze-coloured Cinema Three offered Warren Mitchell in *Moon Zero Two*. The present aluminium panels on the front of the building were fitted at this time.

REGENT Abbeymount

The Regent was built for local owner F.R. Graham-Yooll, opening on August 1st 1927. Its main front was formerly Younger's St. Anne's brewery and the architect of its conversion into a cinema was T. Bowhill Gibson. Despite the unusual site he had to work with, this is Gibson at his more conservative, although the entrance to the auditorium is still dramatic, the patrons at one time entering below one corner of the screen.

Managed by W.S. Albin, the new cinema had a thirty-foot stage, a tearoom, and a Compton organ which brought queues to hear visiting organists like Leslie James or the resident performer Richard Telfer, later music master at George Watson's. In the Forties, live concerts are believed to have been given in combination with the Capitol in Leith; by that time both houses were owned by Gaumont-British. The Regent's musical connection continued into the Sixties when Mrs. E. Lamb won a top award in the Odeon and Gaumont Festival with her Boys' and Girls' Club Choir.

The Regent closed with *Carry On Again Doctor* and Oliver Reed in *The Trap*, on May 2nd 1970. The occasional Fringe show has been performed there, but the building is now derelict.

Regal Interior before tripling

Dog matinee at the Regal, 1958

The Scotsman

RIO/COUNTY 16 Wauchope Avenue, Craigmillar

The Rio, designed by Linton and Grierson, opened on February 6th 1936 with Dick Powell and Ruby Keeler in *Flirtation Walk* and Edward G. Robinson in *Passport to Fame.* It was owned by M.E. Broadhurst and seated 1,100 according to the *Cinema Buyer's Guide.* However after only ten years operation the cinema was hit by fire, its stalls, circle, and gallery being completely destroyed in a blaze on October 5th 1946. The proprietors by that time were H. Paulo and Robert Scott of the County, Portobello, who then commissioned none other than T. Bowhill Gibson to reconstruct the cinema. A new house called the County emerged on August 29th 1950, opening with Robert Paige in *Red Stallion* and Donald O'Connor in *Feudin, Fussin, and a'Fighting.*

The last picture show at the County featured Gerhard Riedman in *Arena of Fear* and Don Borisenko in *The Fast Ones,* on October 18th 1963. The building still stands as a bingo hall, its sparse exterior a monument to the inspiration of Art Deco.

RITZ Rodney Street

Built by Scottish Cinema and Variety Theatres, which was later to form the nucleus of the ABC chain, the Ritz was designed for both silent and Talkie films. In the event, Talkies reached Edinburgh during its construction so the new Rodney Street house opened only for sound. "The step the directors have taken" commented the *Evening News,* "is a courageous one". The cinema was described as "somewhat futuristic" and "exceedingly bright" with heavy carpeting to deaden noise. Much ado was made about the luxury of a tip-up seat for every one of the near-2,000 patrons.

From the start the Ritz had a famous manager in Jimmy Nairn, who was previously at the Savoy, but who stayed five years at Rodney Street before making his name in cinema

Ritz, Rodney Street

management in Inverness.

The Ritz opened on September 10th 1929 with *The Singing Fool* only a few months after the cult film had left Princes Street. According to the *Bioscope* magazine the opening was made with little fuss, although the first patrons were shown a film of the building, made by Nairn himself. In its post-war days the Ritz shared programmes with the Regal, bringing first-run films to a house which might not otherwise have aspired to them. However the end came on November 28th 1981 with *Exorcist II* (*The Heretic*) and *Mad Max* — a sad comment on the change in public taste. Applications for a bingo licence had been consistently refused. The sound blister put in for early Talkies was for long visible on an external wall but the building was demolished in 1983.

RITZ KINEMA (Morningside) *See* SPRINGVALLEY CINEMA

ROXBURGH 1 Drummond Street

The Roxburgh Hall in Drummond Street gives little hint that it was once a cinema, yet it opened as the Roxburgh on New Year's Day with William Faversham and Barbara Castleton in *The Silver King*. Seating 550, its most interesting feature was the built-in plaster screen. As the cinema did not advertise regularly its closure date is not known, nor is there any record of it becoming a Talkie house. The opening of the New Victoria must have hastened its end.

ROXY *See* POOLE'S ROXY

ROYAL CINEMA *See* TRON

RUTLAND (GAUMONT) 4-8 Canning Street

The Rutland supercinema was built by the General Theatre Corporation, possibly with the involvement of F.R. Graham-Yooll. It was opened at the west end of Canning Street and the east end of Torphichen Street, on April 23rd 1930. Its opening show was *The Loves of Robert Burns* featuring a former local boy, the St. Mary's Cathedral chorister Joseph Hislop. Besides the films, the Rutland's attractions included Lyndon Laird, doyen of the city's cinema organs, on the "mighty unit organ" and Norman Austin with the Rutland Symphony Orchestra. The decor was worth seeing too; two thousand lights were used for interior decoration in variations of orange, silver, and light blue. The seating was old rose and two medieval panels flanked the screen. These were intended to be removed if the screen needed enlargement. All this was the work of T. Bowhill Gibson, designer of so many Edinburgh cinemas. Seating 2,187 patrons, the Rutland immediately made it into the city's "big five", but it closed on April 4th 1950 after showing *Sand* and Loretta Young in *Come to the Stable*.

The cinema reopened only two days later as the Gaumont with Larry Parks starring in *Jolson Sings Again*. The two side pay boxes had been replaced by a circular one and a padded leather advance booking office was installed later. The Gaumont was a Rank cinema with its seating reduced to 1,700 but when fire broke out on May 30th 1963, the cinema was doomed. In applying for permission to demolish, Rank pointed out that there were five supercinemas within walking distance and permission was granted on June 26th 1966. The Gaumont's last picture show was *A Pair of Briefs* and Hardy Kruger in *Taxi to Tobruk*.

Gaumont

ST. ANDREW'S SQUARE CINEMA Clyde Street

The St. Andrew's Square cinema was another daring venture on the part of the Edinburgh financier F.R. Graham-Yooll, whose family company were builders' merchants and oil manufacturers in Leith. Despite its name, his new cinema did not occupy a place in St. Andrew's Square but was tucked away in nearby Clyde Street on the site of the former Royal Dick Veterinary College and a Baptist chapel. Seating 1,500, the cinema opened with Harold Lloyd in *A Sailor-made Man* on January 1st 1923. To build in a side-street was a dangerous step for a publicity-dependent enterprise like a cinema so Graham-Yooll gave out a mass of complimentary tickets and hired an orchestra leader from London. Under Sam, the St. Andrew's Square orchestra attracted long queues to its Thursday evening orchestral interludes. The cinema was sold to Gaumont-British before 1929.

When the Talkies came to Princes Street, the St. Andrew's Square cinema advertised itself as the "Home of Eloquent Silence" but on October 21st 1929 started talking with *King of the Khyber Rifles* — "a tale of the 42nd Highlanders" to be heard as well as seen "with the latest and most up-to-date sound installation". But it was typical of the technical uncertainty of those early Talkie years that other equipment introduced the following April was "a decided improvement".

This cinema suffered an unplanned fate common to many of its kind: on November 12th 1952 the St. Andrew's burnt out. Fire had started in the projection room, a fireman almost being killed when the roof collapsed. Locksmiths in nearby St. Andrew's Street also escaped when a falling wall demolished part of their workshop. Although the impressive reinforced concrete balcony survived the fire, the owners were faced with a £300,000 bill to rebuild the cinema and instead sold the site, which is now part of the bus and coach station. The last show comprised *Gentle Gunman* (John Mills and Dirk Bogarde) and *Young Paul Baroni* (Richard Rober and Bruce Cabot).

ST. BERNARD'S PICTURE PALACE *See* SAVOY

SALISBURY 38 South Clerk Street

This building was formerly the Livingstone Mission Hall but opened as a cinema on December 17th 1925 showing the imperishable adventure romance *The Sea Hawk* by Rafael Sabatini. The Salisbury was owned by the well-known P.S.L. Lucas, whose name recurs frequently in the story of the capital's cinemas. Unfortunately the cinema was hit by accidental fires and partly destroyed on February 14th 1939 and again on January 22nd 1943. The films showing in the latter half-week were *I Killed That Man* starring Ricardo Cortez and *Highway West*. It is believed that the cinema did not re-open because of an understandable failure to secure insurance cover, but this is unconfirmed. The building was then used by C. & J. Brown as a furniture store and later absorbed into the firm's premises.

THE SALON 5 Baxter's Place

The Salon opened on October 2nd 1913. Its first patrons must have been either horrified or delighted to be greeted by male staff in turbans, while the female attendants sported nautch dancer costume. Hence the immediate nickname "The Harem". The decor had a Persian theme and there was a tea-room. The Salon's owners were Regent Photo Playhouse Ltd. and the first show included a version of *The Lady of Shalott*. Seating capacity seems to have been between 800-1,000.

Perhaps surprisingly the Salon survived the decline in cinema attendances in the Fifties and Sixties showing mainly second-run westerns. It actually outlasted the neighbouring Playhouse by about a year, until November 1974, when the Salon's proprietor E.D. Lonie applied for permission to turn the cinema into a pub. The last picture show was *The Dirty Heroes*

(Marcello Mastroianni) and *Tenth Victim* (Ursula Andress). The building is now derelict but its fate seems to be linked with the architecturally important houses behind it. Unfortunately, unlike the Playhouse, the Salon is unlikely to make a Phoenix-like appearance on the Edinburgh entertainment scene.

SAVOY (TUDOR) St. Bernard's Row, Stockbridge

This was probably the site of an organ-builder's establishment and later a billiard saloon before it opened as the Palace picture house on April 10th 1911, the first show including film of the Scotland v England football international at Ibrox. A year later the cinema had been renamed the St. Bernard's Picture Palace. In 1914 the managers calmly told the *Bioscope* magazine "no opposition is to be faced in this part of the town" and made the special claim that sloping flooring in the cinema guaranteed the patrons an uninterrupted view of the screen. On March 28th 1921, when showing D.W. Griffith's *Hearts of the World,* the cinema changed its name to the Savoy.

From 1925 it had the good fortune to be managed by Jimmy Nairn, later manager of the Ritz and one of the most highly-respected personalities in the cinema business. He remembered the Savoy as a small (seating around 920) dingy house with a three-piece musical ensemble, of which only the lady pianist would remain after 10.30 p.m. Nairn later admitted that he had expected a more modern example of a Scottish Provincial Variety Theatres cinema. In 1960 the cinema was renamed yet again — this time as the Tudor. Its last picture show was on April 23rd 1966, showing Gregory Peck in *The Guns of Navarone.* The Tudor was demolished in 1982 and replaced by an apartment building with (or is it imagination?) just a hint of theatre architecture on the roof.

LA SCALA (CLASSIC) 50 Nicolson Street

Ralph Pringle, one of the great cinema pioneers in the North of England and in Scotland, opened the La Scala Electric Theatre on December 31st 1912. Previously the site had been occupied by a riding school, a circus, and a theatre, the last-named reputedly built from stones from the Zoological Gardens. The theatre establishment comprised the New Royal Alhambra (opened in 1862) and the Royal Princess's Theatre (closed 1886), the latter being famous for its pantomimes. Between the closure of the theatre and the opening of the cinema, the auditorium was the setting for Salvation Army services.

By 1914 the La Scala was a theatre-cum-cinema showing occasional variety turns but films ran on the continuous system from 6.30 to 11 p.m. It later passed into the ownership of Peter Crerar, owner of a small cinema chain in the Thirties. Its change of name to the Classic on April 27th 1974 indicates that another change of ownership took place, with the new proprietors introducing "adult" films.

Whether erotic films are to your taste or not, the Classic is still one of the most interesting cinemas to visit. The balcony is now closed, reducing capacity to 294 seats, but still carries "PR" monograms in gold, while the words "Princess Theatre" have only recently been obscured in the present entrance. The building can claim to have one of the longest entertainment pedigrees in the business.

SCOTIA *See* HAYMARKET

SILVER CINEMA *See* LYRIC

Tudor/Savoy

Kevin & Henry Wheelan

Springvalley, Morningside

SPRINGVALLEY Springvalley Gardens, Morningside

This could be called the cinema of many names. It began as the Morningside Public Hall when Springvalley Gardens was built around the turn of the century. Before that the site housed cow byres for a local dairy herd. The cinema's names included the Morningside Photoplay House, the Ritz Kinema, Evans Picture House, Cine Playhouse and (for the Twenties and Thirties) the Springvalley Cinema. There appear to have been three proprietors over this period — R.M. Ireland in 1914, Thomas Butt thereafter, and George Murray probably from 1934. The Springvalley closed in 1938, three weeks after the opening of the Dominion. It then became what the Post Office Directory mysteriously calls the "Del. Mar. Hall" and from about 1939 it was the Silver Slipper Ballroom. It is now a wholesaler's warehouse and little of the cinema survives, although the frontage is largely unchanged.

THE STAR 16 St. Mary's Street

St. Mary's Church Hall still stands in St. Mary's Street but only the existence of a former projection room hints that this used to be a fairly notorious cinema for up to fifteen years after 1914. The hall appears to have opened in 1878 and was used for drama, boxing displays, and the early meetings of Hibernian F.C. However from about 1914 it is listed in the *Kinematographic Year Books* as belonging to Wilson and Wilson and/or the Star Picture House Company. Thus it received the nickname of "The Starry".

Remembered with affection as a pennygaff, the Starry is said to have accepted jam jars as an admission fee, although this habit is often inaccurately attributed to smaller picture houses. In those days when even the Princes Street houses smelled of carbolic, managers used disinfectant liberally to maintain hygiene standards. Legend has it that the Star's ushers

State

Kevin & Henry Wheelan

regularly squirted syringes of disinfectant along the backs of the cinema's seats because of the male patrons' distressing habit of relieving themselves without leaving the auditorium!

The Star is listed in the *Year Books* until 1929 but its last picture show may have been as much as five years before that date.

STATE North Junction Street, Leith

The State was a luxury supercinema, Edinburgh born and bred. Opened on December 19th 1938 by the Miller, Albin, McLaughlin group, the cinema even had a Scottish-produced sound system (Shearer-Horn), although the Holophane lighting system was an import. Part of a complex including four shops, two billiard saloons and a skittle alley, the State had a local architect, Sir James Miller, who put a variety of shapes into this cinema. The pillars are flattened ovals in cross-section, the splendid entrance hall (walnut panelled and once gold) looks as if it should have twelve sides, but five are taken up with the curve of the doorway. Stairs plunge and bend towards the auditorium, which the visitor should imagine in its original green, silver, and ivory. The roof includes a kind of pagoda structure and the cinema's dramatic position over the Water of Leith makes the kind of building the imagination hastens to find a use for. Solidly sited, its stanchions go down twenty feet to get below the level of the river's bed.

The State's first show was in aid of its near-neighbour, the Leith Hospital. The programme included Madeleine Carroll and Henry Fonda in *Blockade* and Gene Autry in *Boots and Saddles*. The last advertisement announced Richard Burton and Clint Eastwood in *Where Eagles Dare* for May 11th 1972. Bingo now reigns in this, Leith's last cinema.

TIVOLI *See* NEW TIVOLI

TOLLCROSS (NEW TOLLCROSS) 140 Lauriston Place

The Tollcross cinema, advertised as "The Distinctly Different Theatre", opened at Hogmanay 1912, on the site of a former slaughterhouse. It was designed for its owner Thomas Stewart by A.L. Goodwin, the city architect who also created the Haymarket. The Tollcross was part of a complex including a billiard saloon and a furniture display room and store. Boxes were reservable in its first year, so it must have had some pretensions to grandeur although some of the seating was at right-angles to the screen. The "Toll-X" was managed by a Mr. & Mrs. Ladley but later passed to the Lucas family, probably when the widowed Mrs. Ladley died.

On January 16th 1943 the cinema reopened as the New Tollcross, renovated and redecorated. Its first film featured Victor McLaglen as *Dick Turpin*. However, the small size of the auditorium boded ill for the cinema and it closed at the first sign of the industry's decline, on September 27th 1947, after showing *Broken Blossoms* and *Mystery of the Riverboat* with a supporting western and Popeye. The New Tollcross was altered for storage of furniture and only the frontage is now visible.

TRON (ROYAL) 235 High Street

Lady Piggott Redford opened the Tron cinema, owned by A. Harris, on April 17th 1913. Its first films were *A Vision of the World* and *From Sky Blue to Purple Deep*. At some point the cinema passed into the hands of the Alhambra syndicate and the Tron last advertised on June 1st 1928: Hoot Gibson in *Galloping Fury*. It reopened as the Royal on December 27th 1928 with *Why Sailors Go Wrong* (Sammy Cohen and Ted Macnamara) but probably closed within the year, unable to adapt to Talkies. Until recently the building was occupied by Alex Sloan and Company and the cinema exits can still be seen.

TUDOR *See* SAVOY

VICTORY *See* BUNGALOW

WAVERLEY 6 Infirmary Street

Little is known about this cinema which was open to the public sometime before the First World War but did not survive the war's upheaval. The Waverley opened on an unknown date in the New Jerusalem Church, originally run by the Edinburgh branch of the Swedenborgian Society. The building is basically a box afflicted with a carbuncle in the shape of another smaller box comprising lavatories. The remains of paint can still be seen adding a top-dress of classical architecture to the structure.

Popularly known as the "penny scratcher", the little picture house did not advertise, and George Baird, the city's first cinema historian, believed that entry could be bought with a 1lb jelly jar. The lucky patron even received a free orange. The Waverley was owned by James McMahon between 1911 and 1920 but by 1922 it was in the possession of Robertson and Hogg, electricians and brassfitters, whose names can still be read there. Presumably the Waverley was a casualty of the shortage of film-staff which broke a quarter of British cinemas in the war to end all wars.

WEST END CINEMA *See* ALBERT HALL

ACKNOWLEDGMENTS

The author acknowledged the help given him in his research by Janet McBain of the Scottish Film Archive, J. McLaughlin, W. Maguire (for assistance and for permission to draw on the Palace Cinema accounts now in Register House), J.K.S. Poole, D. Cameron, E.M. Lucas, Sadie Aitken, the Cinema Theatre Association, and the staff of the City Libraries' Edinburgh Room.

The publisher wishes to acknowledge the *Evening News's* permission to publish quotations from this newspaper. Among others who assisted with information after the author's untimely death in August 1983 were Francis Canning (who unfortunately died in February 1984), Richard B. Lacey, Francis Reid, and Kevin S. Wheelan. Thanks are also due to Bill Brady and Richard Wilson of Scotsman Publications.

As well as providing a popular history of Edinburgh cinemas and cinema-going, the publisher hopes that this book will be a small memorial to the late Brendon Thomas, greatly missed by his family and many friends.

FURTHER READING

An indispensable aid to the cinema history researcher is George Baird's three-volume typescript on Edinburgh's theatres, circuses, and cinemas, in the City Libraries' Edinburgh Room. Other works consulted by the author were:

Atwell, David: *Cathedrals of the Movies.*

Cant, David: An Introduction and Conservation Assessment of the architecture of the Nineteen-Thirties in Edinburgh. (Typescript, Edinburgh School of Art/ Heriot-Watt University).

Edinburgh Film Guild: *21 Years of Cinema: a 21st anniversary retrospect of the work of the EFG.* (Edinburgh, EFG, 1952).

Field, Audrey: *Picture Palace: a social history of the Cinema.*

Kinematograph Year Book

Low, Rachael: *The History of the British Film.*

Mellor, J.G.: *Picture Pioneers.* (Newcastle: Frank Graham)

Morrison, Christine D.: *The Dominion Cinema.* (Typescript).

National Council of Public Morals, Cinema Commission of Enquiry: *The Cinema, its present position and future possibilities.* London, 1917.

Nisbet, Robert: *Theatres and Halls in Scotland.*

Sharp, Dennis: *The Picture Palace and other buildings for the Movies.*

Rockets galore at the Capitol, Leith

The Scotsman

Alhambra Interior — auction of fittings August 1959

The Scotsman

Index

Caley — an early interior shot

The Scotsman